Prai

'*Fly Higher* is the best book I've read for a long time. The balance of humour, personal reflection and self-help is spot on. Not only is it hard to put down, but the techniques can easily be implemented in your daily life from the word go. Outstanding!'

— Mark Keen, Head of International Stakeholder Engagement USVF, Defence Infrastructure Organisation

'A Masterclass in writing a book that is well crafted, honest, thought provoking and highly addictive!'

— Natalie Maddox-Hussain, Commercial Lead, Defence Digital, and Events Lead, Defence Women's Network

'I love the humility and humour in this book. Sarah helps us move from feeling that we're not enough to implementing practical top tips around the power of practice, the importance of sleep and, ultimately, flying higher! A must-read for extraordinary everyday women and men.'

— Harriet Green OBE, global business chair, founder and philanthropist

'Gripping, real, honest and fun, this is personal development for people who don't like personal development. Utterly Brilliant."

— Dr Andy Cope, bestselling author and happiness researcher

'*Fly Higher* gives the reader a fascinating opportunity to consider how much more easily we could deal with life's challenge by making better choices, focusing on what's important and understanding our mindset. Sarah Furness's excellent book helps the reader combat the difficulties and enjoy the highlights of the human condition.'

— Mark Gallagher, Formula 1 executive

'This book is smart, witty and straight-talking: like being told the secrets to success by the coolest, wisest friend. Meditating over a glass of wine and living life unapologetically sounds like the best possible way to be.'

— Natalie Barton, Digital Communities and Marketing Officer, Propertymark

'*Fly Higher* is a penetrating, funny and inspiring book whose alchemy is combat, compassion and choice.'

— Andrew Turner, Air Marshal and Deputy Commander, RAF

'Presented in an engaging, no-nonsense style, *Fly Higher* is essential reading for those of us who wish to better manage our inner critic. Packed full of practical and science-based advice, this book will help you retrain your brain to navigate the full maelstrom of life.'

— Russell Poynter-Brown, Management Consultant and Performance coach

'Since reading this book, I have actually changed one of my terrible habits of flitting between about sixty different jobs thinking I am being dead clever and getting shit done by multitasking. This morning I have set the goal of concentrating on what *needs* to get done in the now, and 'ping' – a bulb has just been lit!'

— Richard Wade, Director, Risk and Safety Compliances Ltd

'A practical and entertaining life hack book born from Sarah's own amazing journey – this is not guesswork! An infectious read.'

— Kay Kennedy, Director, Kennedy Executive Recruitment

'As a former combat helicopter pilot, Sarah has certainly taken the right-hand seat in her approach to a career as a life coach. This book, based on Sarah's experiences, and backed by academic research, is very much a companion manual for mindful living.'

— Nigel Whittaker, Air Safety Manager, MOD

'We cannot all be superhuman, but we can all be super humans. In this book Sarah has captured the true meaning of being mindful and what it takes to perform under pressure. She smashes some business myths, is brutally honest about her own thought processes and failings, and guides the reader through simple but highly effective tools to help ordinary people be extraordinary. This isn't a story about helicopters or combat missions, but a story about how everyone can fly high, remain focused and complete their own personal missions.'

— Dr Lee Williams MBA, [Coach/Speaker], [JOWSA Consulting Ltd]

'Mindfulness and military service are two things you would not imagine being together in the same book. However, Sarah successfully combines mindfulness techniques with her experience as an RAF helicopter pilot to produce a practical guide on how to deal with the stresses and strains of modern life – along with some pretty darn cool stories as well.'

— Andrew Speirs, founder, Lens Digital

Train your mind to feel
as strong as you look

Fly
Higher

SARAH FURNESS

R^ethink

First published in Great Britain in 2022 by Rethink Press (www.rethinkpress.com)

For my mother, Helen,
who taught me to be brave.
And for my son, Arthur,
who taught me everything else.

Contents

Introduction

'No Sarah, I disagree. You *are* superhuman.'

That's what the Men's Radio Station presenter said to me during a recent interview. I was sharing my ideas about how we cultivate mental toughness and had casually dropped in that I was a helicopter pilot in the RAF for twenty years and had served in Iraq and Afghanistan. He then suggested that a helicopter pilot's version of mental toughness might be somewhat out of his normal listeners' league.

I disagree.

The fact is, this lovely man was wrong. I wasn't born different. I'm just the same as you. And that's on a good day. On bad days, I feel like a total fraud. I'm thinking, 'You obviously have no idea what I'm really like if you are saying those nice things. I'm nothing like you, because I'm not as good as you.' I *want* to be the same as you.

So let me be upfront. This book is not about setting me apart from everyone else. It's not about a hero sharing hero stories. It's not about swinging the lantern and telling endless flying dits. If you like the sound of flying stories then rest assured there are plenty of anecdotes in here, but they aren't the point or the driving force behind this book. Part memoir and part training manual for the mind, this book is about connecting with you through the human experience and the rawness and messiness of life. It's a place for me to candidly channel my experiences into one place. To share everything I've learned so that you can feel utterly bombproof, no matter what the world throws at you. Having been to war (both literally and metaphorically) I have some experience in dealing with curveballs, and that's important because it means I know these methods work. But it's also so much more than that. I'm also going to show you why the brain responds the way that it does in adversity and then, crucially, how to train your brain to respond differently in crisis.

On this journey, you will learn why the brain often does things which helps absolutely nobody (especially you) and how to train your brain to perform and thrive under fire. Following the seven steps in this book to retrain your brain to perform optimally under extreme pressure will help you to perform at your best, feel bombproof in adversity and lead with gentle courage. The book focuses on:

- How to understand the mind, particularly when 'under threat'

- How to train and ultimately rewire the mind to feel in control and resilient in adversity

- How these techniques have been used and proven in combat scenarios and flying missions

- How to leverage these skills to relate to others and lead others skilfully and authentically

Do you ever feel hostage to the battlefield that is in your

head? Do you sometimes experience self-doubt, self-pity or even self-loathing? This book is perfect for you if you have high standards for yourself, and others. If you typically get described as strong or confident, but often don't feel that way. If you worry about letting others down. If you sometimes act in a way that you later regret. If you lie awake beating the crap out of yourself for falling short of your own high standards. If you sometimes upset people that you love. If you wonder why the people that you love upset you. If you ever ask yourself, 'Why did this happen?' If you feel like you must have all the answers...

In other words, if you experience fear, anxiety, stress, loneliness, anger or grief, then this book is perfect for you. This is not a book written for robots. This is a book written for humans who experience the full maelstrom of life and secretly hope they might deserve a bit more. This is the book I wish I'd read twenty years ago.

I *did* want to be superhuman, by the way. When I was five years old, I was obsessed with Supergirl, so I constructed an obstacle course in my garden. I was convinced that if I got myself fit enough, I could teach myself to fly. I believed that if I could work up the courage to launch myself off the washing line that I'd be airborne. I never did have the courage to try (mostly because I was terrified of what my mother would say if I broke her washing line). But I *did* learn to fly. And not in the sense you may think.

Imagine we are all swans. You probably know the adage about how swans look graceful on top of the water, but underneath they are paddling like buggery. Well, that's where we will start. Because that swan is you. And just like that swan, there will be times when the conditions are rough. Life will throw in hand grenades that will turn everything upside down. It will seem crushingly unfair, and you might feel like you are drowning or that the world is just downright dragging you under. This is the crucial 'sink or swim' moment when you can choose to keep swimming. That's what you're going to learn in this book. You're going to learn how to swim in the choppiest of conditions, and because you are a swan, you'll make it look easy. In fact, it is easy when you know how.

One day, you'll realise you don't need to keep swimming, because swans can also fly. Not too far from now, you'll spread your wings and take your rightful place in the sky. I'm the proof. Because I'm just like you.

Come with me on this journey. Learn how to navigate through everything weird and wonderful that life throws at you with all your human frailties and limitations. Discover how to come through it all. Smiling. Laughing. Flying.

Choose to fly. And fly higher.

1

You Have A Choice

Do you remember the days when you could impulsively book a flight to Dubrovnik while drinking sundowners in Leicester Square? You could turn up to the airport with sunglasses, your passport and a hangover and then fall into the nearest youth hostel on arrival a few hours later. Or maybe you'd decide not to book anywhere to stay and operate the 'pull or die' philosophy.

There were no amber lists, red lists, passenger locator forms, Covid-19 vaccination passes, pre-booked lateral flow tests. I don't remember ever checking the Foreign and Commonwealth Office advice before travel. I don't remember waiting anxiously to be 'traced' on return from my holiday to see if I could leave the house. I just went straight to the pub to show off my new tan. Travel was footloose and fancy free (at least that's how I remember it).

Then the 2020 Covid-19 pandemic struck and all of that changed. Suddenly there were *rules*. Lots of them. And paperwork, which you had to fill out in triplicate and include the precise details of your holiday (even down to which toilet you would be using, in which restaurant and on which day). It seemed that navigating your way through an airport or attempting to board an aeroplane was just an excuse for some official to tell you which rule you were currently breaking.

I was on a Turkish Airlines flight back from Dalaman when I wrote this. They had just served us a limp sandwich and informed us that people sitting in the same row were not to all remove their masks at the same time. We were to take it in turns to eat our lunch. Despite the fact that I was sharing a row with two people I live and eat with every single day, of course we complied. It was preferable to suffering the embarrassment of a public telling-off by the air steward.

I'm not saying this to have a go at the powers-that-be. I understand that these rules had been put in place to keep us safe. And what a wonderful world we live in where we have lots of people devoted to exactly that – keeping us safe. I'm certainly not suggesting I could have done any better. (Well, maybe a bit better.) But it does highlight an interesting challenge that is central to this book, and the subject of this chapter. Choice. Or more accurately, the apparent lack of it.

I think it's fitting, as the sun sets on the Covid-19 era, to reflect on what it's taught us about choice. What has really struck me is this: we all pretty much followed the rules. (Yes, I know there were some rebellions against the rules, but by and large I think we are a pretty obsequious bunch.) By following the rules, our choices became limited. Indeed, many felt that our choices had been taken from us, but most of us cooperated. That tells us a lot about how the human mind works.

At some point, we've decided it's easier just to go along with it rather than become a disrupter, and then, bit by bit, we give away all sorts of other choices. We blindly follow our sat navs (metaphorically not literally). We pick up the sweeties at the counter, not considering that whoever designed the store layout essentially made that choice of confectionary for us. We get diverted by some meaningless TikTok meme that popped up in our feed, which, if you've watched the Netflix documentary 'The Social Dilemma', you'll know was deliberately planted in your feed at that precise moment with the sole purpose of selling you more useless rubbish. Which means Mark Zuckerberg is choosing what we buy online for us. We wear the latest fashions, so our clothing choices are dictated by the editors of the latest fashion magazines.

The science behind choice

This is not your fault. The brain accounts for a whopping 20% of energy consumption, despite being only 2% of our overall body weight, so its default will always be to conserve as much energy as possible.[1] Our neurons (pathways in the brain) are inherently lazy. For any given situation, our brain uses all its senses to gather information about that event, then decides what to do and sends signals around our bodies to help us implement our chosen course of action. The first thing it does is ask, 'What did I do last time?' As long as we are still alive, our previous response is deemed good enough and no further

---

1   ME Raichle and DA Gusnard, 'Appraising the brain's energy budget', *PNAS* (July 2002), www.ncbi.nlm.nih.gov/pmc/articles/PMC124895, accessed 26 May 2022

analysis is required. What is the upshot? We no longer need to choose our next move. We can just react instinctively.

While there are clear evolutionary advantages to this brain functionality, such as energy consumption and time, we would do well to understand what this means for us. We are hardwired to react, *not* to think. This means that not only are we giving away our choices, but we probably don't even realise we have them in the first place.

So what's the problem? The truth is, usually none of this causes a problem for us. Culture, past experiences, other people's behaviour, upbringing, relationships, environment, threats – they all shape our choices without us realising most of the time. And most of the time we get by perfectly well. Until we don't. Until we start delegating important choices that result in us living in conflict with our values. Until we can't discern between external influences and our own internal compasses. Until we take on someone else's narrative as if it were our own, and then wind up feeling confused, misunderstood and a failure.

While my mother was still alive, I would consistently baffle myself at the moody teenager level I would descend into the moment we started interacting. It didn't seem to matter how many pep talks I gave myself. Something about the way she breathed just got me angry. I couldn't seem to help myself. She'd ask me some eye-rollingly stupid or annoying question that was utterly beneath me and then sit there, mouth open, waiting for a response. The vitriol that used to come out of my mouth makes my stomach turn when I think about it. And because I'm not actually evil, of course I'd feel like a monster afterwards. Does that ring a bell?

Have you ever uttered the words, 'Adam/Sheila/John [insert name as appropriate] brings out the worst in me?' I'm sure there is someone you can bring to mind. There are two valuable clues in that statement:

1. The word 'worst' implies we don't like the way we behave around this person. In other words, our behaviour in that scenario is counter to our values. My guess is, just like me, you probably feel ashamed of your behaviour and wish you'd reacted differently. This doesn't make either of us weak or evil. It just means we have some healthy values (for example, one of my go-to values is, 'Don't be a dick'), and we've contravened those healthy values. It happens. Welcome to being human.

2. Let's pause to reflect on 'brings out the worst'. This indicates that in some way we feel like we've behaved against our will. We've attributed the cause of our behaviour to someone else. In the example of my mum, it was the 'stupid' question that triggered me, or maybe it was just her breathing with her mouth open. Attributing our bad behaviour to someone else is quite normal, especially when we feel a bit embarrassed because we've behaved like a dick. (I mean how much of a dick do you have to be to get annoyed at someone for breathing?) Pointing the finger at someone else has the short-term appeal of being able to deflect the blame away from us, but in reality, we're effectively saying that someone else makes us behave a certain way. And that's simply not true. Nor is it helpful. If we continue on this trajectory, at best, we will end up in conflict with our own values and fail to realise our full potential. At worst, we will start to find ourselves loathsome. Trust me on this one.

If you are only going to read one chapter of this book, read this one. In this chapter I'm going to share a secret that changed my life. It is amazingly simple, yet easy to overlook – so easy in fact, that I overlooked this small but important fact for the first forty years of my life. When I finally had my eyes opened, nothing was ever the same again. The discovery I made was this: you *always* have a choice.

That's right. No matter how many uninvited curveballs get thrown at you, no matter how many pointless government regulations you have to follow, no matter how many cringe-worthy family birthday parties you feel you have to endure, no matter how impossible it may seem to do things the way you want to do them – you always have a choice. I'm not saying you have all the choices. I'm not saying you own the whole universe and can decide everyone's fate on a whim; nor am I saying that shitty things won't happen that you didn't ask for. And I'm certainly not saying that you somehow deserve or brought about those shitty things. Life is tough. Stuff goes wrong. All the time. But no matter how criminally unfair life may appear, I promise you, you *always* have a choice.

The secret is your response. You get to choose how you respond to life's hand grenades. You get to choose how to interpret the things that happen to you. (Don't worry if you don't realise that yet, we'll get to it shortly.) You get to choose if something will be the making or the breaking of you. You get to choose what to do next, even if it's simply, 'What superhero pants am I going to wear today?' (I'm a big fan of Batman pants.) You always have a choice. You can choose how to interpret any given scenario.

Let's break down the annoying mum scenario again. I told you that she asked a stupid and annoying question. She probably asked me something like, 'So Sarah, when are you going to get pregnant?' in response to my gripping war story about how I flew into a landing zone under fire and saved thirty-seven orphans. Now, I'm sure a lot of us can relate to how annoying that sort of question might be. Let's list the reasons why this question would initiate the red mist in me:

- I don't really know the answer to that question because I'm not God.

- I'm wondering if she was even listening to my war story, because I was really hoping to impress her.

- I'm thinking all she cares about is an heir and not my service to Queen and country.

- I feel inadequate because I was not rewarded for my service by an immediate pregnancy.

- I still find her breathing quite annoying.

For all those reasons, I am irked by this question and my reaction is to come back with some cutting remark which leaves her in no doubt as to her inadequacy as a mother. (I'm pretty good at cutting remarks.) But let me ask you something:

- Who made the judgement that the question was stupid? I did.

- Who decided that my mum should be more interested in my flying stories than seeing the birth of her grandchild before she dies? I did.

- Who appointed my mother as the person who needs to be impressed by me and make me feel worthy? I did.

- Who decided that I am inadequate for not being pregnant? I did.

- Who chose to find her breathing annoying? I did.

I'm not saying it's not natural to respond this way. The important point is that I am the one who is choosing to interpret that question in that way, and it's usually because of my own insecurities.

Exercise: ABC

Draw the table below on a piece of paper or in a notebook. Now recall a scenario when you behaved in a way you are not proud of. Take some time to understand *why* you responded the way you did. This is not designed to make you feel more shame – I've just shared the fact that I was a bitch to my mum who is now dead and who I can never apologise to, so trust me, there is no judgement here.

Now complete each of the boxes. And don't beat the shit out yourself. You're being brave by doing this.

At First	Behaviour	Consequence
What thoughts and feelings come up?	What did you do?	What did you think and feel afterwards?

I'll be brave too and share my own example of this exercise:

At First	Behaviour	Consequence
Mum: 'Sarah, when are you going to get pregnant?' My thoughts: 'Why doesn't she care about my service? Why is she being so insensitive about my failure to get pregnant? She should be proud of me.' My feelings: irritated, (subsurface) ashamed.	Snapped at my mum.	My mum got huffy and I felt indignant at first, then awful.

Our brains will search for the meaning of everything we experience. That is the principal purpose of our thoughts: to interpret what happens so that we can react appropriately and stay alive. It was thoughts and feelings that triggered the behaviours above and, by becoming aware of how we are choosing to interpret something, we can start to realise just how much agency we have over what we think and feel.

Now it's tempting to think, 'But I can't help what I think and feel. Why would I choose to be upset by something someone said?' And this is a great point. There are lots of times it doesn't feel at all like a choice, so let's dig a little deeper.

Thought one: 'I'm inadequate because I can't get pregnant.' This is a great example of me taking on someone else's narrative without even realising it. In this scenario, I was probably comparing myself to my friends who were married at

27, already owned their first house and had, by now, produced 2.4 children and bought a dog. I am feeling inadequate compared to them, but this means I'm living in accordance with their narrative. In turn, perhaps they are living in accordance with their neighbour's narrative, who had their first child when they were twenty-six. And of course, there is the age-old biological clock which strikes fear in the heart of all 30-somethings – but it only strikes fear because we've been told about it. It's important to note that I'm not saying it's irrational or wrong to think these things, simply that we should realise our thoughts are being shaped by other people. Which is fine most of the time, but not when it is causing us to feel shitty or behave like a dick.

Thought two: 'My mum should be proud of me.' This is probably because she spent her whole life telling me I was brilliant, so I learned to expect it. I learned to bask in it. I learned to use it as my yardstick for self-worth. I learned to trust her judgement about *my* worth over my own. We now know that there is a problem with giving our children too much praise for precisely this reason. It can actually cause performance anxiety.[2] Who knew? This is why most of us are afraid of failing, which, paradoxically, makes us afraid of success. It's not because our parents and teachers were trying to mess with our heads. They were just doing what they thought was right, but either way, we've taken on the value to measure ourselves by other's standards and that is exhausting and a battle we're sure to lose.

---

2   R Coe et al, *What Makes Great Teaching?* (Sutton Trust, 2014), www.suttontrust.com/our-research/great-teaching, accessed 9 June 2022

Now, I want you to think about these external influences and add them into the melting pot of learned behaviours (because that's what they are), and then I want you to remember what I said about lazy neurons. They take the path of least resistance. For any given situation, the first thing the brain asks is, 'What did I do last time? Did I live through it? Great. I'll do that again.' And again. And again. So the trigger-thought-behaviour pathway starts to become ingrained, and ta-dah. You have a learned behaviour which then becomes automatic.

What does all this mean? It means those thoughts that have been shaped by other people, our society, our upbringing, etc, have led to behaviours that are taken on as our signature behaviours. Those thoughts which have essentially been chosen by other people are influencing the kind of person you are showing up as. You are allowing other people's choices to define who you are. You are giving your choices away.

Becoming choice aware

Still with me? Good. The purpose of this revelation is not to make you feel stupid. Remember, your brain is just doing what brains do. The purpose is to show you just how often you have a choice in the first place, even if you unintentionally gave that choice away. That's actually great news, because it's by becoming choice aware that we can start exercising that choice in a way that actually serves our values.

This doesn't require much reflection beyond this chapter. We don't need to spend years in therapy understanding *all* the ways we have been influenced to show up this way. We don't have to spend hundreds of pounds lying on a chaise longue getting angry at our parents for not having all the answers. It's enough to know that we are influenced by all sorts of things, that our thoughts and behaviours carry the blueprint of everything that has gone before us, and that this is normal.

In a nutshell, if you've been showing up as a bit of an asshole to date, you can forgive yourself. Thus far it's not really been your fault, because you didn't know you had a choice. That's about to change. It is true that thoughts will pop up unbidden, so to that extent we don't get to choose what we think, but we do get to choose how we engage with those thoughts:

- **Option A:** We choose to take them as incontrovertible facts which must be acted upon the way we always act on them.

- **Option B:** We choose to treat them with some good-humoured scepticism and then decide what we are going to do next.

 Write down which option you would choose

This is the first and most important choice you will ever need to make. Did you write Option B? Good – I knew you'd be awesome.

Now, here's what's next. The first thing you need to learn is how to become aware of when those unbidden thoughts pop up (ie when you are not consciously choosing what to think), because that is the moment when you are most likely to give that choice away. Distraction is a useful combat indicator of how often you give away your choices. When you are distracted by something, you are not consciously choosing where to focus your attention; you are being diverted to a particular train of thought by something or someone else. It could be something popping up on your phone. A sudden noise. An ache in your shoulder. A flashback to a pointless phone call with a utility company – I've recently moved house so I can list lots of examples here. Just like that, your attention is somewhere you didn't choose for it to be. Let's try it.

Exercise: Noticing how often you don't choose what to think

· Give yourself the task of focusing on your breathing for the next minute.

· Count your breaths from one to ten.

· Every time you notice that your attention has wandered away from your breath, simply resume your counting at one and start again.

· Do this exercise for one minute.

· What was the highest number you got to before you got distracted?

On average, you will usually get to about two or three breaths before you notice that you've started:

• Daydreaming

• Planning

• Ruminating

- Feeling bored

- Insert your own distraction here

Research by two Harvard psychologists showed that we spend around 47% of our waking day distracted.[3] How crazy is that? The good news is, every time you notice you have become distracted, you are becoming choice aware. You are *exercising choice*. You can start to hone this awareness of how often you are distracted as an indicator of how often you might give your choices away. The reality is you are going to get distracted no matter how much you try not to be – that's just how brains are. Thoughts and feelings are still going to pop up out of nowhere, so you don't need to fight this, but you do get to choose how you engage with these. Take the example of your phone pinging. You can't stop the fact the phone just pinged and you were distracted, but you can make a choice: you can pick the phone up and become absorbed in whatever the evil social media giants are trying to sell you, or you can notice the distraction and then turn your focus back to what you were doing before.

The same is true for thoughts that pop up. You get to choose to take them as incontrovertible facts that you must immediately act on the way you have always acted on them, or you get to choose to treat them with some good-humoured scepticism and then go back to what you were doing. The point is, you don't always choose for these thoughts to pop up, but you can choose whether to be at the mercy of them. Now you might

---

3   N Klemp, 'Harvard psychologists reveal the real reason why we're all so distracted', *Inc.* (2019), www.inc.com/nate-klemp/harvard-psychologists-reveal-real-reason-were-all-so-distracted.html, accessed 26 May 2022

say, 'But how is that possible? When these thoughts pop up in my head, I feel like there is no escape. If it was that easy to leave them be, I'd just do it, so why can't I?' Simple, really. Up until now, you probably didn't realise you had a choice, so you weren't practised at choosing how to engage with your thoughts, feelings and distractions. But you absolutely can choose, and what's more, it's easier than you might think.

The simple fact is that the cognitive thinking brain can't be in two places at once. You cannot give your attention to more than one thing. Think about when you are at a dinner party and are in conversation with someone across the table, but you're also trying to eavesdrop on what your partner is saying to someone else. Or you're on a Zoom call while secretly emailing your colleague. Take a moment to think about if that's even possible. And if so, how? It's possible because you are switching from one object of focus to the other. That's why, when you're listening to two people, you have to tune in to each one separately and therefore miss a crucial point in your partner's conversation. When you're emailing during a Zoom call, you inevitably miss part of the Zoom conversation (and Sod's law says it will be when you are asked a question). It's also why you don't always hear what someone else is saying, because you get lost in your own thoughts, perhaps triggered by something they just said. In this instance, your attention is on your thoughts and not what the other person is saying.

This might appear like a limitation – your distinct lack of ability to see and hear everything all at once – but actually it's a saving grace. If you are focusing on a task, even if that task is simply counting your breaths, you cannot be focusing on whatever self-sabotaging thought just popped up. And here's the good bit: because all your thoughts and feelings are transient, no matter how angry/sad/scared you feel right now, you don't feel that way forever. When you stop giving your focus to those thoughts and feelings, something magical happens... They fade away. By deciding to focus your attention somewhere that you choose, those unwanted thoughts will diminish.

Making choices that serve you

I'm not saying that these thoughts won't return, and it's not to say they won't repeatedly pull for your attention, but every time you notice you are distracted by a thought, you can simply repeat the process: choose where you want your attention to be, and repeat the process as often as you need to. If this sounds weirdly familiar, it's because this is the classic distraction technique that parents use on their children. Distract your child with a fun task and they will forget about their broken tractor. It is equally effective all the way through adulthood. The only reason we don't use it is because we've either forgotten that we can, or because we have prescribed to this pop-culture of deeply introspective theorising and analysis where we feel the need to understand the origin of our thoughts, wrestle with them and ultimately conquer them. In my opinion, the latter is an unnecessary use of valuable energy and has the potential to retraumatise, keeping us stuck in the past. The solution, if you ask me, is far simpler. Notice the thought and then give yourself permission to focus on something else. Every time you do that, you are making a choice that serves you.

Now of course it is easier said than done. Not least because neurons are lazy (remember) and like to do what they did before, so don't lose heart if this feels like a mammoth task to start with. But I promise you, it can and will be done. You just need to commit to training your mind to focus your attention where you choose and then go ahead and start doing it. Little by little. Every time you choose where to focus your attention, you are taking charge of your brain and rewiring those neural pathways. Every morning from now until say, forever, before you reach for your phone (or whatever else you instinctively reach for, no judgement here), try this exercise.

Exercise: Seven mindful breaths

- Close your eyes, inhale and focus your attention on where you feel the breath in your body. Notice your chest expanding. Notice the cool air entering your nose.

- Now exhale. Notice how your chest contracts and the warm air that's in your nose or mouth.

- Every time you notice you are distracted (whether it's thinking, planning, remembering, external noises, aches and pains...), notice it without giving yourself a hard time, and then bring your focus back to your breath.

- Repeat seven times.

That's it. You have just started training your mind and becoming the boss of it. Go you! You can do this with your kids too. Put a teddy or a favourite book on their tummy and just ask them to focus on the movement of the object.

There is a parable in a famous Buddhist text called 'The Dart'.[4] Basically, a man is struck by a dart. He feels great physical pain (as one would expect). He now has a choice: he can roll around on the floor focusing on his pain and misfortune and get struck by a second dart – the psychological dart – or he can acknowledge his pain without becoming distracted by it, thus avoiding the second dart. The moral of the story? We don't always get to choose what happens to us, nor do we choose to be distracted by unwelcome thoughts or feelings, but we do get to choose our next move.

Initiating the simple practice of choosing where to have our focus helps us to consciously exercise choice in our lives. We can, for example, choose to focus our attention and energy on things we have little direct influence over (weather, other people, news), or we can instead choose to focus our energy and attention on things we can directly influence. Examples of this include, but are not limited to, our behaviour, how we respond to adversity, and how we engage with our thoughts and feelings. We will be learning more about this throughout this book.

Key takeaways from Chapter One

- We *always* have a choice.

- We can choose how to interpret our experiences.

- We can choose how much attention to give to unpleasant thoughts and feelings.

---

4   N Thera, 'Sallatha Sutta: The Dart', translated from the Pali by N Thera. *Access to Insight, BCBS Edition* (13 June 2010), www.accesstoinsight.org/tipitaka/sn/sn36/sn36.006.nypo.html, accessed 26 May 2022

- We can only focus our attention on one thing at a time.

- We can choose to use our attention as a 'force for good' by focusing on what nourishes us.

- Every time we focus our attention where *we* choose to (eg the breath), we are training our minds to be more 'choice aware'.

2

Stop Multitasking

I remember the first time in my RAF career that I thought I was going to die. We were flying in a formation of helicopters at a low level through a steep-sided, winding valley. When you fly at low level (about treetop height), there are quite a few things you need to avoid hitting:

- The ground

- Other aircraft

- Birds

- Cables and wires

Believe it or not, electricity wires are pretty much invisible to the naked eye when you're flying at 120 knots. You need to look for pylons to spot wires and avoid them. When you are down in the valley, the pylons are often above you on the ridgeline, meaning you have to keep an eye on the map, so you know where to look for them. This is why we need to practise low-level flying so often. It's high risk and there's a lot to think about, so it requires high levels of competence. It's also terrific fun.

On this day, I was flying through a valley in Morocco. There was a small mountain road that wound itself around the valley sides and I remember saying (perhaps a little arrogantly), 'If a car can get round it, so can a helicopter.' My instructor chuckled and replied, 'I think I might tighten my harness for this one.' What happened next, happened incredibly quickly.

We were all having a great time and then my instructor, who was in the seat next to me, suddenly shouted, 'Fuck!' The canopy shattered and then everything got noisy in the cockpit. I immediately realised we had hit wires and was certain that these wires would now be wrapping themselves around my tail rotor. I'd seen the videos of what happens to helicopters when their tail rotors fail, and I knew that spinning into the ground at 100 G was imminent. I remember dreamily thinking, 'So this is how I'm going to die,' and feeling quite pleased it would all be over quickly. Then came four words I will never forget.

'Fly the aircraft, Sarah,' my instructor shouted. And just like that, my attention was back in the cockpit.

The view from the jump seat seconds after we hit high-tension electricity cables in Morocco

Why am I telling you this story? Well, because I want you to be impressed by my bravery of course (I joke), but seriously, this story is the perfect vehicle to demonstrate why multitasking is literally the worst idea the twenty-first century has ever had. If you remember nothing else from this chapter, please let these words sink in: your attention cannot be in two places at once.

The reality of multitasking

We cannot multitask. That's right, just when you thought multitasking was the thing that was allowing you to keep smashing those work tasks out of the park, I'm afraid I've got bad news for you. Multitasking actually decreases our productivity, takes more time out of our day, impacts our decision-making, makes us more stupid and increases our stress levels.[5] Seriously. I am not making this shit up. This is all backed by science, and to demonstrate it, I'm going to ask you to do a little exercise. You'll need a pen, a notebook or piece of paper, and a stopwatch.

Exercise: Where is my focus?

I'd like you to write 'Where is my focus?' in your notebook on two lines like the example below. Time yourself doing this.

Where is

my focus?

---

5   K Cherry, 'How multitasking affects productivity and brain health', *verywellmind* (July 2021), www.verywellmind.com/multitasking-2795003, accessed 26 May 2022

Now do the same exercise again, but this time, I want you to switch from the top line to the bottom line after each letter. Write *W* and then go down to the bottom line and write *m*, then up to the top line and write *h*, and then down to the bottom and write *y*, and then up to the top... You get the idea. Time yourself doing this and reflect on the following:

- What differences did you notice?

- How long did each exercise take?

- What was the standard of writing on each?

- How did it feel to complete the task the second time?

These are the typical results of the second part of the exercise:

- It takes longer.

- You have to really think about it.

- You space out the lettering or use capitals to make the task easier.

- Your standard of writing decreases.

- It can feel stressful, though some people find it quite enjoyable.

Why? Well, here's the science bit.

The science bit

MRI scans have shown that when we try to do two things at once, the brain tries to split itself into two (the logical, problem-solving cortex and the more primitive and jumpier survival 'chimp' brain) and delegate one of the tasks to the 'automatic' part of the brain. For this to be possible, one of those tasks needs to be something we can do without thinking about it. For most of us, writing is a task we don't have to think about too much, but if I make the task harder, so that both tasks require input from the cognitive part of the brain, we must do something called 'task switching'.[6] We modelled this when we switched from the top line to the bottom line in the last exercise. When the brain has to switch from task to task, it is having to use cognitive functions to activate task switching and 'rule activation processes'. For example:

- **Task switching:** 'I'm now switching from writing an email to reading a notification that's popped up.'

- **Rule activation processes:** 'The rule for writing an email is that I use a QWERTY keyboard so that I know where to position my fingers to type, and the rule for reading a notification is that I look at the top right of the screen and read from left to right'.

The brain will do all of this in the background, but the penalty of using some of its cognitive bandwidth is around a 40% decrease in performance. (This can be illustrated by the reduction in the standard of your writing in the little exercise.) Now relate that to other tasks. If that's an email to your boss asking for a raise, you may have misjudged the tone, or the 40% decrease in performance could lead to an increase in errors. You've now got typos in your email. Is that something you can afford?

---

6   KP Madore and AD Wagner, 'Multicosts of multitasking', *Cerebrum* (2019), www.ncbi.nlm.nih.gov/pmc/articles/PMC7075496, accessed 26 May 2022

It also takes a finite amount of time for your brain to carry out these background tasks. We are talking microseconds here, but studies show that this adds up to a whopping 2.1 hours each day.[7] To put that into context, every time you are distracted from writing an email by, say, a notification popping up, it takes your brain about a minute to get back to where it was when it was distracted. You know the 'Now where was I?' routine – if you add all those minutes up, you get to over two hours. Imagine if you could find a way to get those two hours back? What would you do with an extra two hours in the day? (Keep it clean people. Actually, don't. Be as naughty as you like.)

If you're still not convinced and are consoling yourself that your brain is getting an extra workout when you multitask, I'm afraid there is more bad news. Extremely clever people (who presumably don't multitask) have undertaken studies to prove that the repeated practice of spreading your attention among competing tasks degrades the brain's resilience and can eventually lead to brain freeze – much like when your computer freezes if you overload it. In fact, studies have shown that task switching while completing cognitive tasks lowers IQ performance by up to fifteen points. This is roughly equivalent to the degradation your cognitive function experiences if you pull an all-nighter. If that isn't scary enough, studies carried out on habitual multitaskers showed that they were poorer at filtering relevant information from irrelevant information.[8]

---

7   C Steinhorst, 'How to reclaim the huge losses that multitasking forces on your company', *Forbes* (Feb 2020), www.forbes.com/sites/curtsteinhorst/2020/02/28/how-to-reclaim-the-huge-losses-that-multitasking-forces-on-your-company/?sh=6d569deec024, accessed 25 May 2022
8   A Hoyt, 'How multitasking works', *HowStuffWorks.com* (February 2017), https://science.howstuffworks.com/life/inside-the-mind/human-brain/multitasking.htm, accessed 26 May 2022

Not only will you have wasted two hours to produce an inferior product, which you'll probably need to spend time correcting, you'll have reduced your ability to prioritise effectively – which probably means you've wasted even more time by focusing your efforts on the least important task.

The final kick in the gut is that multitasking activates the stress response. When your brain is dashing from one object of focus to the other this simulates a 'multiple threat' environment and the fight, flight or freeze system kicks in. When this happens, the brain prioritises information from its survival cells and effectively shuts off the prefrontal cortex. The prefrontal cortex is the part of the brain responsible for regulating emotion, problem-solving, creativity and storing long-term memory. With this effectively 'de-activated', you cannot access these functions when your stress response kicks in. This is why you find it hard to 'think' under stress, why you forget simple things ('What's the word again, it's just flown out my brain?!') and why you can't think laterally or field challenging questions – until ten minutes later when your brain reveals the perfect solution to you, and you kick yourself for standing there frozen to the spot. It's not your fault. Your brain is simply doing what it is designed to do by activating the freeze response in the presence of a threat. Tell me, do you really need that extra stress in your life? You don't.

In case you think you do, I've got an answer for that too. For people that found this exercise fun or believe that stress is helpful – this paragraph is just for you. The common objection I often get at this point is that some people genuinely believe they thrive under stress. They think that stress can be positive. This is not their fault. The language is confusing.

We commonly talk about stress when what we really mean is distress. When we talk about positive stress, we are really talking about eustress – positive feelings of excitement and satisfaction.

The best way to explain this is by looking at how our performance peaks and troughs relative to the cortisol levels in our body. The chief purpose of cortisol is to put us into a state of arousal. Snigger all you want (I did), but seriously, cortisol is what allows us to wake up in the morning. It's what's responsible for the wide-eyed, heart-thumping, wake-up jolt we get when we start to feel drowsy at the wheel. It's what switches on our fight or flight reaction and makes us super-alert in the presence of danger. Without cortisol, we'd probably be dead, which shows that it's *not* the meanie we make it out to be. If there are low cortisol levels in our system, we will get bored, switch off, underperform or even fall asleep. Many studies have been done on this but the simplest one (and my favourite), is the Yerkes-Dodson curve.[9]

You'll see from this curve that there is a peak in our performance when cortisol rises, but just a little bit more cortisol and our performance nose-dives. If we want to maintain optimum performance, we need to sit just under the apex. This sweet spot is commonly referred to as 'stretch', and those of us who profess to liking a bit of stress are really referring to this stretch zone. This is when we are in *eustress*. This is when the magic happens. Make no mistake, though, when we hit the distress zone, it's all downhill. Literally and figuratively.

---

9   A Pietrangelo, 'What the Yerkes-Dodson law says about stress and performance', *Healthline* (Oct 2020), www.healthline.com/health/yerkes-dodson-law#how-the-law-works, accessed 26 May 2022

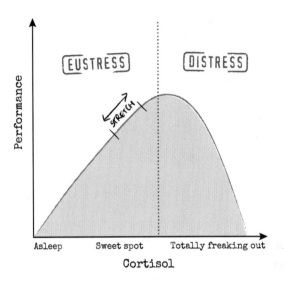

The Yerkes-Dodson curve

Bottom line: We can get away with multitasking when the tasks are 'natural', don't drain the prefrontal cortex and can be done reasonably automatically, eg washing the dishes and listening to the radio. Unfortunately, in our current culture of doing everything 'right now' and an underlying sense of urgency and immediacy, there is the increasing potential for 'mission creep'. A benign secondary task might now be substituted for something more critical, eg emailing your boss, texting a grieving friend or driving down a wintry road at night. Multitasking is not just over-rated – it's positively dangerous.

Multitasking in practice

Let's go back to Morocco. Hopefully by now it's obvious why my instructor wanted me to focus on flying the aircraft. If my attention could only be in one place, then it needed to be in the one place that mattered. It needed to be on flying a badly damaged aircraft, not my eulogy. When I reflect, I realise this is exactly what our training was designed to do. It was designed to equip us with a well-practised ability to focus on *one* thing and to be damn sure that the one thing was the most important thing.

You might think on first inspection (as I did) that flying training is about honing our ability to multitask. Indeed, flying training often involved instructors throwing multiple injects (objects/challenges) at us. During one of my test flights in the Hawk (the jet that the Red Arrows fly), I was once asked to perform my aerobatic sequence while telling jokes – I think the best I could come up with was, 'What's the equivalent of half an orange? The other half.' This style of training does feel a lot like multitasking, except we had this mantra: 'Fly the aircraft.' We were taught that no matter what else was going on, we were to always make sure the aircraft was flying in a straight line first, and then, when it's all trimmed out (which is a bit like hitting cruise control in your car), we would have the capacity to turn our attention to the next most important considerations, such as, 'Where am I going and how do I get there?' Then, when those questions were answered we could turn our attention to the next most important thing, eg 'Who do I need to talk to on the radio? What am I going to say?' And so on. We called it a 'work cycle' – it was a way of prioritising where to focus our attention and allowing ourselves to focus on one thing at a time, one after the other.

All that training. All that being messed around by our instructors. It wasn't just because they were sadists (not all of them, anyway). It's because they were training us to prioritise which task to focus our full attention on. We were training to have our attention in one place. You can't train yourself to multitask. Career mums can't do this. Jet pilots can't do this. Movie directors can't do this. I should know – I've tried all three.

You can train yourself to prioritise, though.

The reasons you will nod, but change nothing

Hopefully you are now on the edge of your seat with excitement, thinking of all the things you can achieve when you ditch multitasking, and yet, no matter how much we know something is a good idea, doing it is a different matter. Why? Well, there are a few reasons. Let's have a look at them.

Your brain will resist you

The first problem is, we have become so accustomed to constant distractions that it has become *neurally* ingrained. Distraction has become our new normal. Did you know that the average person touches their mobile device 2,617 times per day?[10] Are we aware that we're doing that? Not 2,617 times a day, we're not. This is not our fault. Remember that the brain is brilliant but lazy, so being distracted by the shiny lights of our mobile phones is perfectly natural. Being distracted is simply an indicator that our brain is on autopilot and doing what it's designed to do. Think about what multitasking is: it's the repeated practice of darting

---

10   J Naftulin, 'Here's how many times we touch our phones every day', *Insider* (July 2016), www.businessinsider.com/dscout-research-people-touch-cell-phones-2617-times-a-day-2016-7, accessed 9 June 2022

from one object of focus to the next. It's literally the opposite of mindfulness. It's a combat indicator of your brain being on autopilot.

I've already explained why being on autopilot can lead us to giving away our power, or of living in conflict with ourselves, but hopefully you can see that autopilot also sets the conditions for multitasking. Yet again, our brain is doing exactly what it is designed to do, but in this case, it's leading us down the garden path.

The good news is, no matter now neurally ingrained something is, we can always train our brain. We start by training our minds to focus where we choose to. In one place. It doesn't really matter what that object of focus is. The important thing is that we are deciding where to focus our attention. When you notice you've become distracted, which is the gateway to multitasking, bring your attention back to where you choose. You already did this exercise in Chapter One, so I'm not really teaching you anything new here, I'm just giving you another reason to practise it. Go ahead, start by renewing your intention to take seven mindful breaths each morning. You are teaching your brain that just because it gets distracted, that doesn't mean it has to stay distracted.

Fear of saying no

It's all very well being the enlightened one, but that's not much help when everyone else around you is still convinced that multitasking is the best thing ever. Open door policies, open plan offices, inclusive cultures – all well-meaning and quite possibly indispensable – are a natural enemy of uni-taskers. Remember that everyone else has got their shit going on too

Exercise: Prioritising your focus on what really matters

The Eisenhower Matrix[11] is useful for this. Draw a matrix like the one below and use it to decide what tasks you will uni-task. These will be the tasks that fit into the top two blocks of the matrix.

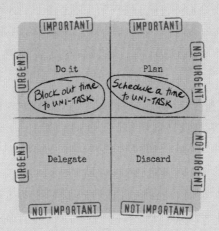

The Eisenhower Matrix

Now determine how to make it feasible for you to uni-task. Write a list of the things you can do to increase your ability to uni-task. Be prepared to be brutal with this. The reality is that a lot of us spend great chunks of time doing things we don't really need to do. Remove as many distractions as you reasonably can. Close the office door, turn your phone and notifications off. Pick the time of day when you are most engaged (for most people, it's first thing). Scheduling breaks will reduce your natural tendency to procrastinate (which is often a covert way to multitask).

11   'Eisenhower Matrix' (CFI, no date), https://corporatefinanceinstitute.com/resources/uncategorized/eisenhower-matrix, accessed 26 May 2022

(and everyone else thinks that their shit is the most important thing in the world), so they are going to expect you to put down whatever you are focusing on and focus on them.

And whether you want to or not, most likely you will. This is not surprising, because at some point you evolved to be tribal, which meant your survival relied on you being accepted by the tribe, which led to you becoming hardwired to please others. Saying no or disappointing others is intensely uncomfortable for most people. But here's a secret that will change your life. Feeling uncomfortable won't kill you. You can say no, and you will survive. The world also won't end if you disappoint some people.

Here is something you can try that will help you to say no politely. If you are interrupted by someone, try having an assertive but respectful conversation. For example: 'I can see this is important to you. I'd like to be able to give this the full attention it deserves. Can we find a time to sit down and go through this together? I have a window between... How does that fit with your schedule?' By using this technique, you are acknowledging what is important according to that person's Eisenhower Matrix, but you are also preserving your own.

Fear of being dispensable

Feel like you're spinning so many plates and yet there's no earthly way you could contemplate dropping one? You tell yourself, 'I have to go on. I simply don't have another option. If I drop a plate, there is no one there to catch it.' I get it. I've told myself the same lie. When I decided to start up a business, I was a home-schooling, single mother and

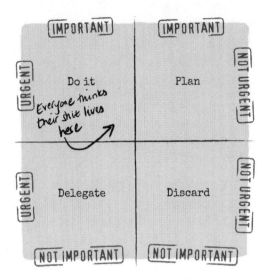

How important is your shit?

still serving in the RAF running a human performance and air-safety school. I was overloaded and I knew it. The RAF kept asking more of me and I kept saying yes. Convinced I couldn't change anything about my work demands, I briefly considered asking my ex-husband to take on more of the childcare. Briefly. But I didn't. (I certainly bitched about it behind his back though.) I remember that familiar thrill of self-importance as I whinged to the fellow home-schooling mums. 'Men just don't get it, do they?'

This is one of the oldest tricks in the book. We convince ourselves we have no other choice, that no one else can do what we do, that we are indispensable. Indeed, there is an odd comfort in this, because then we don't feel foolish for running around after everyone like a headless chicken. But the truth is, the people around you are often extraordinarily capable of working their own shit out... Provided you let them. Provided you can give yourself permission to be dispensable. Think about the 'assertive conversation' technique we've just covered. A work colleague may come to you convinced you need to help them right now. If you politely but firmly explain you can see them in a couple of hours, guess what usually happens? They work their shit out. Not only have you now relieved yourself of an unnecessary task; you've helped them to grow and become more self-reliant. It's a win-win. (We'll visit this again in Chapter Seven.)

Fear of being alone with our thoughts

Living in a frantic world has become perversely addictive. Not only do we revel in how busy we are – which hopefully you can now see is just a reflection of poor prioritisation or a fear of saying no – it also gives us a convenient excuse not to sit alone with our thoughts for too long. People often comment on their inability to meditate because they 'just can't empty their minds.' We seem to think we must either be running around full throttle juggling a million balls or living in a cognitive vacuum. Neither are feasible. There is only one way to empty that mind and the good news is, it's coming for all of us. Death. Until that point, thoughts will keep on coming. That's what brains do.

The benefits of uni-tasking

If the thought of focusing on only one thing is freaking you out and you're thinking, 'How will I get all my shit done?' then I've got some good news for you. Let's go back to flying training. To start with, if my instructors asked me to make a radio call *and* fly straight and level, the result would be me and the aircraft upside down somewhere on the approach path for Newcastle, while swearing over the airwaves. But over time I got better. Why? (No, it's not because I got better at multitasking. Sorry, not budging on that one.) It's because after hours and hours of training, certain actions become automatic. Recall what I said earlier: We get away with multitasking when they are 'natural' tasks that don't drain the prefrontal cortex and can be done reasonably automatically, eg washing the dishes and listening to the radio. (Yes, I did just quote myself.)

It's said that a monkey can be taught how to fly – and I'm the proof of that. Over time, I developed the ability to operate the radio *and* keep the aircraft in a straight line. Sometimes I even managed to navigate to the correct airport (go, me) because I didn't have to think about flying the aircraft. You see, given enough practice, even flying a multimillion-pound aircraft will become muscle memory, which effectively means the brain doesn't have to think. Technically, therefore, you're not multitasking. But you are achieving two things at once.

 Write a list of things you could do concurrently which do not require you to multitask.

Here are some of mine to get you started:

- Walking meetings
- Listening to a podcast on my commute

- Taking my son to his favourite cafe to play while I write this book

- Combining the school run with my daily exercise

Alternatively, you can also do just one thing and achieve multiple benefits. Here are two of my favourites.

Sleep

I could write a whole book on the wonderful outcomes of sleep, along with the disasters that await when we decide to forgo it. I don't have to, because Matthew Walker has already written *Why We Sleep: The New Science of Sleep and Dreams*.[12] If you have a particular interest in sleep, I highly recommend you add this to your reading list. According to Walker, here are just some of the benefits that a decent night's rest affords us:

- Deep sleep is essential for us to transfer short-term to long-term memory, so sleep is crucial for learning and assimilating new information. This is why cramming the morning of an exam can actually be a bad idea, because it sort of scrambles our memory.

- Sleep allows us to process traumatic events. There is something kind of magic when we sleep. We can relive an event, but the 'emotion' is taken out of it. The expression, 'Time is a great healer,' should probably be corrected (in my humble opinion) to, 'Sleep is a great healer.'

---

12   M Walker, *Why We Sleep: The New Science of Sleep and Dreams* (Penguin, 2018)

- This is further illustrated by the discovery that the hormone responsible for dumbing down this emotion overnight wasn't present in those diagnosed with post-traumatic stress disorder. Hence why those affected keep having flashbacks. Their brains are desperately trying to process the trauma, but they don't have the necessary hormones to facilitate it. It's also why bad dreams are not an indicator that we are all fucked up beyond repair. Bad dreams are our brain's way of healing from unpleasant experiences, so sleep is basically free, overnight therapy.

- Sleep also improves our ability to 'read' facial expressions. When we are tired, we are more likely to read facial expressions as threatening and think that the world is out to get us when that is most likely not the case.

- Sleep improves our ability to use 'System 2 thinking' (ie the prefrontal cortex), which means we are better at creative thinking and problem-solving. It is said that Edison used to deliberately wake himself just after he'd entered REM sleep to access the 'lightbulb' moments of creative thinking.

Sleep is a wonderful example of *one* thing we can do with our time that has multiple benefits. If you are already sold on the benefits of sleep but find it elusive, you are in good company. Post-Covid, I have noticed many of my clients reporting poorer sleep. This leads them to think that something is wrong, yet the opposite is true. This is yet another indicator that our brains are doing exactly what they were designed to do in a world that is obsessed with the 'busy' narrative. That is to say, the chief reason why we don't sleep is an overactive amygdala, because we have too much cortisol coursing through our bodies. If we are hijacked by an overactive amygdala, the simplest thing we can do is soothe the threat system through some mindful breathing.

There are several books and courses dedicated to getting a better night's sleep, but you can start by looking after the basics: exercise, fresh air, having a wind-down routine, sleeping in a cool dark room – all of these can help us to get a good sleep. If you couple some of these techniques with the mindful breathing we have already discussed, you might surprise yourself at how quickly you drift back to sleep. Try this meditation as you start your wind-down routine.

Meditation: Winding down

Read through the following instructions several times or follow along with the guided meditation on Soundcloud at https://soundcloud.com/user-978445649 – 'Wind down'.

- First, take a moment to check in with any thoughts, just noticing their quality and any judgements. Give yourself permission to let all that go for now.

- Focus your attention on your breathing, gradually increasing your exhale and slowing your breathing rate down.

- Breathe in for four counts and then out for six counts. Take a few moments to practise your longer exhale, just slowing down your breathing rate.

- If you get distracted by thoughts, that's totally normal. Just bring your attention back to breathing in for four, and out for six.

- Now turn your attention to your body.

- Scan down from your head to your toes, starting off at the crown of your head.

- Scan down your forehead and then your nose and your cheeks.

- There is nothing special to do here, just observe as you scan down through your neck and your shoulders.

- If you notice that you're holding any tension, imagine breathing into that area and then letting go of any tension as you breathe out.

- Continue scanning down through your spine, your chest and your hips.

- Now down the thigh bones, through the shins and into your toes.

- Imagine your body and breath fusing together, breathing into your whole body.

- Keep your breathing relaxed. Take deep breaths and then gently allow your body to relax and release any tension as you exhale.

- Have a lovely big breath in, feeling the warmth as your whole body expands.

- Now release a final, relaxed breath as you let go of the last bit of tension and ready yourself to relax and wind down at the end of a busy day.

Mindful listening

Let me tell you why this is one of my favourite exercises. When we listen mindfully, we hear the *whole* conversation. Think about when you are trying to tune into two conversations. You can't do it, can you? You have to switch from one to the other, which means you'll be missing bits from each. The same is happening when you're tuning into your own thoughts. You are missing nuances, expressions, intonations or even words that are being expressed. We've got used to this, in fact, sometimes we even celebrate it – couples will remark that they 'finish each other's sentences.' This is seen as an indicator of how well they know each other, but it's probably more accurate to say they are focusing their attention on making assumptions about what the other will say and not listening as fully as they could. And then we wonder why we feel misunderstood, or that people just don't 'get it'. The upshot of distracted listening is we miss things which can cause confusion, or perhaps worse, the need for repetition, which can bring stress to the relationship.

The counter to distracted listening is to give your full attention. Here are the multiple benefits that can be enjoyed from this one activity:

- You get a much fuller and better understanding of what the other is saying.

- You save time by not having to correct faulty assumptions.

- The other person feels truly heard.

- The relationship flourishes.

- You are focusing your attention in one place, so you are training your mind to focus and uni-task.

- You are learning to acknowledge and sit with a busy mind. (This is a ninja skill that we will return to in Chapter Five.)

Practising mindfulness is *not* about clearing the mind, it's about seeing the mind clearly and not fighting with it. There is nothing wrong with us having unsettling or difficult thoughts, and as we will see in Chapter Five, sometimes they can be rather useful. When we can sit with something, it no longer holds as much power over us, so being able to accept these unsettling or difficult thoughts is a valuable skill to have. In the meantime, it's enough to understand that it's perfectly natural to resist sitting quietly with our thoughts. The next time you have a conversation with a colleague or loved one, set your intention to listen with your full attention. (It might be useful to tell them you are going to try this exercise.) Here's an exercise you can try which will introduce the skill of mindful listening.

Exercise: Mindful listening

- Now that you are fully focused, notice the words they are using, notice the pitch of their voice and its volume. Also notice their body language.

- If, after a while, you become distracted by your own thoughts, understand that this is quite normal. You will often stop listening so that you can think about what you are going to say (or do) next.

- Similarly, you might find yourself making assumptions about what the other person is saying, and again, this is just what busy minds do. Whenever you notice this happening and your thoughts become distracted, simply bring your attention back to what the other person is saying, how they are saying it, and focus on their facial expressions.

- When they have finished speaking, you may need to take some time to gather your thoughts, so there may be a silence. It is quite normal if this feels a little uncomfortable.

- Allow yourself to sit with that silence before you speak.

Key takeaways from Chapter Two

- Multitasking reduces our performance and increases our stress.

- We can train our brains to uni-task to achieve better results and save time.

- The biggest barrier to uni-tasking is fear of saying no and fear of being dispensable.

- Having respectful and assertive conversations with work colleagues about the importance of uni-tasking can help to address these fears.

- We can achieve multiple benefits from doing one task, for example, mindful listening because we are training our brains to uni-task, communicating better and improving relationships.

3

Train Hard, Fight Easy

In 2018, Charlotte Worthington was working in a kitchen rolling burritos in Manchester.[13] She became interested in BMX riding, particularly pulling stunts. She dedicated all her available time to training and in 2021 went to the Olympics in Tokyo. Charlotte had two runs in which to impress the judges. On her first run she totally wiped out and the whole crowd winced. Then the reigning champion and favourite for gold, an American girl Hannah Roberts, did her second and final run. She punched the air with joy. Hannah had done a fantastic routine. It was a gold medal performance, and everyone knew it, including Charlotte, who now sat on the top of the run about to do her final routine. Her face was hard to read but she looked surprisingly composed.

Then Charlotte did something no other woman had done before. She pulled off a 360 backflip. She won gold. And she made history. I remember watching it, thinking she might have been deterred in the face of such opposition and decided

---

13   'Charlotte Worthington' (Team GB, no date), www.teamgb.com/athlete/ charlotte-worthington/3litzT475zrY443PmCwejH, accessed 26 May 2022

to retire gracefully. When Charlotte was later asked how she had maintained her composure and been able to go back out there after her previous wipe-out and Hannah's performance to pull off such an unbelievable feat, her response was simple. She said that she'd just had to have faith that all the work she had done had been ingrained into her body. And that is exactly what we will be talking about in this chapter. How we train ourselves to keep cool under pressure, and maybe make history at the same time. (We may as well aim high.)

I once coached a team GB boxer. He asked me the same question that many others have asked since: 'Did mindfulness give you the edge in combat?' I remember searching my brain for some eye-wateringly cool story. You know, the one where you're under fire, maybe taking a stray bullet, shouting, 'It's just a flesh wound,' as you emerge from a burning building carrying three wounded SAS soldiers and then single-handedly flying them to safety in a badly damaged chopper. I have no such story, sadly. Of course, I have been shot at. A few times in fact, but sometimes I didn't even know about it until I landed. Bizarrely, the first time I saw tracer fire I thought someone was setting off fireworks. I remember thinking, 'Ooh, that's pretty,' until I heard my co-pilot shouting, 'Contact,' over the radio.

So, on first inspection it appears that there is no correlation between all these mindfulness exercises that I've been asking you to do and your ability to become a superhero. If I wasn't even aware of some of the danger I was in, you could argue that mindfulness did not give me an edge – but I knew that it was the key. I knew that mindfulness could help me to become a superhero. I just had to find the link. And I did.

Practise, practise, practise

There is a reason Charlotte trusted that she could pull off a 360 backflip after a spectacular wipe-out in front of the whole world. There is a reason why I was able to stay focused on flying the aircraft while I was under fire. There is a reason why you will be able to head into your own battlefield and not melt into a puddle of goo. Charlotte used the word herself: ingrained.

To be able to make sound decisions under pressure, when your threat system is on red alert, those decisions must be ingrained, automatic behaviours. For these behaviours to become ingrained, we need to train, train and train some more, and we do this in 'peacetime' so that we can fall back on this training during 'conflict'. At the time when we need it most, sound life-or-death decisions will be instinctive, we won't have to consciously think or decide, because our brains will already know what to do. We will have trained them.

It is pointless doing this training when we are under stress. Remember, our primal brain takes over and initiates a fight/flight/freeze response in the presence of a threat. As we discussed in Chapter Two, it is at this point that the rational prefrontal cortex gets circumvented. The brain is prioritising fast reactions over conscious, philosophical debate. And, because the amygdala works on a 'better safe than sorry' principle, it is prone to exaggerating the threat. Basically, our amygdala is designed to produce strong emotions that are so unpleasant we feel an irresistible urge to do something now. In the absence of rational thought, our brain will default to whatever we did last time. Training our brains to learn new, ingrained behaviours when we are under stress is a pointless exercise, but the good news is, we can train our brains to be less reactive and to recover more quickly from stress. We can also develop new and more helpful learned behaviours to default to under stress. I like to call these **H**ealthy **A**utomatic **B**ehaviours **I**n **T**hreatening **S**cenarios – HABITS. (Like what I did there?) Here's how…

Training our brains to be less reactive under stress

It has been scientifically proven that regular mindfulness practice actually *decreases* the size of the amygdala (the threat centre of our brain).[14] This means it will be less reactive in threatening situations and is less likely to hijack the prefrontal cortex (the thinking, rational part of your brain). Mindfulness also increases and strengthens the connections between these two parts of the brain, which allows better communication between them when you are under threat.[15] The first bit of good news is that every time you do those mental sit-ups (mindfulness exercises) you are making yourself less of a stress head and a bit more Bond-like. The crucial reason why this is so effective is because the brain learns best when it's not distressed. The optimum conditions for training the mind are when we are under low to medium pressure (eustress), and because mindfulness is not a natural state for the mind to be in, this provides a near perfect amount of 'pressure' to ensure we are training our mind when we are on our A-game.

---

14   TRA Kral et al, 'Impact of short- and long-term mindfulness meditation training on amygdala reactivity to emotional stimuli', *Neuroimage* (2018), www.ncbi. nlm.nih.gov/pmc/articles/PMC6671286, accessed 26 May 2022
15   R Wax, *A Mindfulness Guide For The Frazzled* (Penguin Life, 2016)

If you're still not convinced, consider for a moment just how much thoughts can pull for your attention, particularly the less enjoyable ones from the inner critic or the worrier who sits on your shoulder. These thoughts pop up well before you are in total meltdown mode. They are the fabric of daily life. Pulling your focus back from these thoughts to where you choose is not instinctive, and it's not even that easy. If it was easy, we'd have all done it by now and there would be no need for this book to exist. It takes practice. Please trust me, making mindfulness a part of your everyday practice is an absolute no-brainer. The 'hourglass' meditation below is a perfect way to ease yourself into mindfulness daily practice. Remember, the aim here is not to berate yourself every time you become distracted. There is no such thing as meditating badly, contrary to what many people think. You are either *noticing* you are distracted or *focusing* your attention where you choose. Either way, you are still practising mindfulness. Go ahead. Try it, and please pinkie-swear to me that you'll go easy on yourself.

Meditation: Breathing space

Read through the following instructions several times or listen to the guided meditation on Soundcloud at https://soundcloud.com/user-978445649 – Breathing space.

- Start the meditation in an alert but relaxed posture, with your eyes closed or gaze lowered. Take a moment to check in with what's going on in your mind right now.

- Do you notice a busy quality, or a sense of ease? What are your thoughts and feelings? There's no need to judge them or get involved in a conversation. Don't label them as good or bad. See if it's possible just to observe those thoughts and feelings with friendly curiosity or perhaps even humour.

- Narrow your focus to your breath. Just focus on each in breath and each out breath, taking this moment for you. There is nothing else to do. Just focus on your breath.

- Now you can widen your focus to your body. Imagine breathing into your whole body, nourishing it with each breath. See if you notice any tension anywhere in your body. Imagine breathing into any parts of your body holding tension and then letting go of that tension as you exhale.

- Just take this moment for you, nourishing yourself with every in breath, letting go with every out breath.

- As you start to become aware with your contact with the outside world and your part in the outside world, acknowledge that you are enough just as you are.

Training our brains to recover more quickly under stress

Hopefully you've bought into practising mindfulness when not under duress. Laying the groundwork outside of the battlefield will pay dividends, but life is still unfair and unpredictable, and we need to know how to calm our threat systems when the shit hits the fan. Luckily, we can do this by following some simple steps, and simple is key here because our brains are not going to be capable of remembering some wildly elaborate self-care plan (think of the fourteen-page birth plan that gets crumpled up within minutes of the first contraction). When we are in distress, our threat system fires our fight/flight/freeze response. The technical term for this is the sympathetic nervous system (SNS), which has several effects on our bodies.

Our heart rate, breathing, blood pressure, muscle tension and tunnel vision all increase, though conversely, our 'rest and digest' system is suppressed. This is why we don't feel able to eat, sleep or have sex when we are highly stressed. Never was a more blatant lie uttered than, 'I'm a lover not a fighter.' If you are being threatened for your life, you will not feel the urge to shag the aggressor. The technical term for *this* amorous state is the parasympathetic nervous system (PNS).

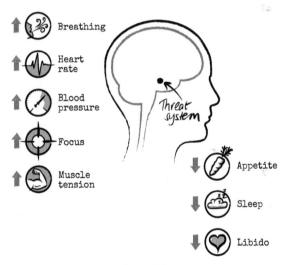

The effects of distress

If we want to soothe our threat system, we need to activate the PNS, and we do that by reversing the trajectories of the SNS. As I said, we need to keep our recovery actions super-simple, so here are some super-simple options:

- Relax your muscles. Wherever you notice you are holding tension (it may be gritting your teeth, a white-knuckle grip, hunched shoulders), notice it and release it.

- Open up your tunnel vision. We tend to get super-focused to stay alert, so you can try just looking around or tuning into the sounds you can hear.

- By far the simplest thing to do is to slow your breathing down. Here are a couple of suggestions you can try:

  - Box breathing: Count in for 4, hold for 4, out for 4, hold for 4. Repeat.

  - 4–4, 4–6 breathing: Count in for 4, out for 4. Repeat 3 times. Then in for 4 out for 6. Repeat 4 times.

The meditation below will also help you to work on your breathing technique. During this meditation, if it feels right, you may choose to walk, pace or even run. This is a great way to respond to stress, because the nervous system is directly linked to the limbic part of the brain when we're in fight or flight. Do what feels right for you. You know yourself best.

Meditation: Cortisol cooldown

Read through the following instructions several times or listen to the guided meditation on Soundcloud at https://soundcloud.com/user-978445649 – 'Cortisol cool-down meditation'.

- Take a moment to check in with your body. Cortisol increases our heart rate, blood pressure, temperature, muscle tension and breathing. See how that's showing up for you right now. Remember, this is a normal reaction to stress. There's no need to judge, just notice.

- If you notice a particular area of tension in your body, imagine breathing into it.

- Continue to focus on your breath for the next three breaths. Count in for four counts and out for four counts, as fast or as slow as you need for this to feel natural.

- Now increase the exhale for the count of six, so take the next three breaths counting in for four and out for six.

- If that feels uncomfortable, you can alter your count. Just make sure that your exhale is longer than your inhale.

- Now check in with your body. Remember where your stress was showing up. Does it feel any different?

- Keep breathing into any areas of tension. There's no right or wrong. Being aware of your physical reaction to stress can help you to react skilfully in the future.

Come back to this meditation whenever your stress triggers or indicators are showing up – and be kind to yourself. All the above are ways of *reversing* the symptoms of your fight/flight/freeze system and activating the rest and digest system. If you do this, you will be deactivating your stress response and by deactivating your stress response, something incredible happens. Because our thoughts, feelings, behaviours and physiology are all linked, as you change your physical state, you will start to think more positively and feel calmer. Honestly, human beings are kind of magic.

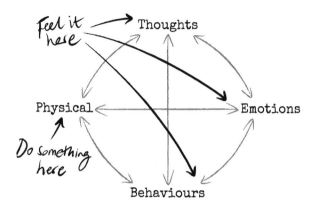

The cognitive framework

Incidentally, this is why people say 'just take a breath' when we are feeling frazzled. Irritating though it may be, they are kind of right. It does help. It won't make all your problems go away, but it will help to reduce your cortisol levels enough to get the prefrontal cortex back in the game. Even if it buys you only a split second in a threat scenario, it's a split second that counts. That split second is enough to give you the space to focus your attention where you choose, and once your System 2 brain (your prefrontal cortex) is back in play, you will be able to access things like emotional regulation and long-term memory. This is how lawyers can remember that complicated legalisation and deliver an ice-cool deposition in court or how a pilot is able to fly a helicopter with a tail rotor failure. It's also why Charlotte, the Olympian, was able to execute a 360 flip on a BMX bike. If you employ the same techniques, not only will you get all the wonderful benefits of lowered cortisol levels, but you will regain the presence of mind to give your full attention to whichever task you are focusing on, so your performance will be world-class. And that's it. That's the secret to being a ninja under pressure.

Now you just need to practise and take charge of your brain. Pull its attention to where *you* want it to be and the easiest way to practise this, is to make it into a habit.

Turning these behaviours into habits

Here's a quick recap. We don't think clearly when we are under threat so, if we want to be able to focus our attention on an object of our choice (for example, our breath), then it needs to become an *ingrained* habit. We need to develop HABITS. But how? There's an art to learning a habit which we are going to cover shortly, but first, let's tackle any misgivings you might have about your ability to learn new things.

Remember when I said the brain is lazy? Our brains will resist anything that requires effort, and learning a new behaviour takes effort. The brain now needs to create fresh neural pathways which, at best, uses a lot of energy which could potentially be wasted, and at worst, our brains will resist making because the new behaviour has not been tested. Our natural impulses won't help us here. We're going to have to grit our teeth and make a commitment to change. (Don't worry, I have cunning ways to make this easier than it may seem right now.)

We've been taught we are either born with talent or we're not, so what's the point in trying to do something we're not naturally good at? But just think about it for a moment. As babies, we are born with literally no ability. In fact, babies are so useless that some people even refer to the first three months of their life as the fourth trimester. At that age, we can't walk, talk or even go to the loo. But have you ever met a fully-grown adult who confesses that, 'Going to the loo is not really a talent of mine; I'll always be in nappies…'?

Do we give up despite constant setbacks? No. Do we eventually learn to walk, talk and wee discreetly behind the neighbours' bushes? Yes (unless there is a profound medical reason which prevents us developing this ability). The sad truth is, as children we learn to be embarrassed or even fearful of failure. We develop a fixed mindset where we'd rather quit while we are ahead than try our best and look stupid. Why? We could blame the results-biased exam system, or the school sports day where we all want to win medals, or our overprotective parents who tell us we are wonderful all the time, making us anxious about losing that praise. (Who knew that praising your child could be such a death sentence for growth?)

If you ask me, it doesn't really matter what the cause is. Nobody set out to make us fearful of change and growth, but the harsh reality is, most of us are to some extent. This leads us to self-consolation. We will say things like:

- 'I'm just not good at cello.'

- 'I've never had an eye for art.'

- 'I've got a short attention span, so if I don't see instant results I lose interest.'

Do you know what all these statements have in common? They are bullshit. Plus, a little saddening, because what we've done with these statements is taken on a setback or challenge as an undeniable part of our identity. What is the truth? Our brains are lazy, but brilliant. We can learn incredible things, provided we put the effort in and stop with the bullshit excuses. Please take this on board. Our parents were right about one thing: we can be anyone we want to be. We've just got to put the effort in.

So how do we create this shiny new habit? I'm going to call this habit 'focusing our attention where *we* want it to be', which is long hand for mindfulness. I could just call it mindfulness, but this is going to make us total ninjas under extreme pressure, so I'm going to call it 'military grade mindfulness'. Feel free to go out and buy a lightsaber in preparation for this new habit.

The components of successful habit creation

There are several stages to forming good habits.

Triggers

These are useful to remind us to practise our new habit. The process of focusing our attention where we choose is not particularly arduous, it's just that most of us forget to even do it in the first place, so it's a great idea to have a trigger reminding us to focus on one thing. For example, if you want to remind yourself to brush your teeth mindfully, you could write something on the bathroom mirror. If you want to remind yourself to go for a run, you could put your trainers by the door. You could write yourself cute little reminders and put them up around your house. It's just about making the trigger accessible.

Just do it

However you decide to practise military grade mindfulness, it's worth noting that the brain will want to procrastinate or try to avoid it. My answer for this is simple. Just do it. Take the first mindful breath. Then go from there.

Reward

The reason we find things addictive is because the dopamine hit we get from doing something never quite satisfies the craving.[16] This is why we need more social media, or more gadgets, or more chocolate. The reverse is true for starting a new, but less instinctive, habit. The reward won't quite seem to match the effort, which is intensely frustrating, but it is how we're wired, so it's pointless focusing our energy on how unfair this is. What we need to know and accept is that our lack of satisfaction presents a challenge to forming a new habit and if we struggle, it's not a sign that we are 'rubbish at sticking at things'. The good news is there are ways to increase the dopamine hit. It's possible to either increase the longevity of the dopamine hit, or the intensity of it. (We will explore some of these methods shortly.)

Lapses

Let me make this clear. Lapses will happen. In fact, they should happen. If it was easy, we would have done it by now, right? But it's not. Lapses, setbacks, mistakes… They are all

---

16   T Haynes, 'Dopamine, smartphones and you: A battle for your time', *SITN* (May 2018), https://sitn.hms.harvard.edu/flash/2018/dopamine-smartphones-battle-time, accessed 9 June 2022

a sign you've got off your ass and put yourself in the stretch zone. Lapses are a sign of progress, not regression. It is fundamental that we understand this if we want to cultivate a growth mindset. Lapses are an essential and inevitable part of habit formation, but we can also use lapses to promote even more growth. (We'll be covering that shortly too.)

Applying these components

I have listed some habits below that you can start to try out. You may notice these are all things you wouldn't normally think about doing – ie they are *automatic behaviours*. These are great behaviours to test your new habit on, because they require you to focus your attention somewhere quite deliberate, a place where you wouldn't normally focus your attention... which is exactly the point. Notice, also, that none of these things take any extra time out of your day so you've got no excuse. I suggest you read through the options below and pick the one you like best.

Mindful eating

Trigger

Choose a mealtime in the day, or a part of a meal that will be your trigger. I like doing this with my dessert as it helps me to slow down and enjoy it. For added benefit, share your intention with a family member or someone you eat meals with. Say, 'I'm going to eat my dessert mindfully so I can really enjoy it.' Once we've shared an intention openly, we are much more likely to go through with it.

Just do it

Notice what your dessert or meal looks like, what colour it is, how the light reflects off it, how it feels in your hand. Smell it. What does your nose and mouth do in response? What flavours are coming up? If it was a blind tasting, would you know what it was? Taste it. Notice how each bit of your mouth responds to it. How your body knows exactly what to do without consciously instructing it. See if you can notice when the after-taste fades to nothing. Notice if you have the temptation to immediately reach for another mouthful before you've finished eating the first. Any time you become distracted by thoughts, you can congratulate yourself for noticing, and then bring your attention back to your food.

Reward

Write down what you notice that you normally wouldn't. Did the food taste better? Notice how much you've eaten versus what you normally would. The longevity of the dopamine hit here is in feeling good for not having overeaten. Notice how you feel having focused on your food rather than the 'to-do list'. Sneaking in some secret mindfulness this way will have reduced your cortisol levels and increased your clarity of mind.

Lapses

If you forget to eat dessert mindfully, then:

- Congratulate yourself for noticing this in the first place. That is awareness and that is mindfulness.

- Remind yourself that lapses are a sign of progress. Another pat on the back.

- Work out what strategy you could try next time. How might you adapt one of the components to make them more effective? Write this down.

Mindful walking

Trigger

If you like walking and find you get lost in thoughts, that's not a problem, but you can make a commitment to spending the first few moments of your walk, practising military grade mindfulness. Again, it helps to write this intention down so that you can hold yourself accountable. You might want to put a reminder on the back of your door or, when you leave the house, deliberately hold your head a little higher than normal so you are seeing above your normal eye-line.

Just do it

Notice five things you can see. Maybe it's different shades of green, different shapes of leaves or the hanging baskets that you normally walk past obliviously. Then four things you can hear. Start close in with your own sounds, your breathing, the rustle of clothing, then the sounds you can hear in the near distance. Follow this by listening for sounds in the middle distance and then go as far out as you can hear. Notice three things you can feel. The contact of your feet on the ground. The feel of the air on your skin. The contact of the wind in your hair. Now find two things you can smell. Perhaps it's freshly laundered clothes or the smell of a barbecue firing up. Then finally, one thing you can taste. This could be the remnants of toothpaste, or coffee or even sweat.

Any time you become distracted by thoughts, you can congratulate yourself for noticing and then bring your attention back to whatever you were focusing on previously.

Reward

What did you notice that you normally wouldn't about your surroundings? How do you feel having taken a break from your frantic mind (while also training it at the same time) Notice how much extra time it has taken out of your day (none).

Lapses

If you forget to walk mindfully then…

- Congratulate yourself for noticing this in the first place. That is awareness and that is mindfulness.

- Remind yourself that lapses are a sign of progress. Another pat on the back.

- Work out what strategy you could try next time. How might you adapt one of the components to make them more effective? Write this down.

Mindful teeth-brushing

Trigger

You could experiment with buying a different type of toothpaste from your go-to or upgrading your toothbrush. Alternatively, if you brush your teeth with a family member, you can share your intention with them. I do this with my son and he's not old enough yet to think I'm weird for saying this.

Just do it

Be curious about how the toothpaste oozes out of the tube, the colours you can see, when you first detect the minty smell. Notice how your body knows instinctively what to do when you brush your teeth. Do you go back and forth or in a circular motion? Do you brush your teeth in a particular order? Notice how the bristles feel against your teeth and gums. Notice the sounds your toothbrush makes. Any time you become distracted by thoughts, you can congratulate yourself for noticing and then bring your attention back to whatever you were focusing on previously.

Reward

What did you notice that you normally wouldn't notice? Pay attention to how you feel having taken a break from your frantic mind (while also training it at the same time). Notice how much extra time it has taken out of your day (none).

Lapses

If you forget to brush mindfully then:

- Congratulate yourself for noticing this in the first place. That is awareness and that is mindfulness.

- Remind yourself that lapses are a sign of progress. Another pat on the back.

- Work out what strategy you could try next time. How might you adapt one of the components to make them more effective? Write this down.

If you've read all these exercises, you'll have noticed a lot of repetition in the words I have used. That's not because I'm being lazy. OK, that's part of the reason, but it's also because the principle behind this practice is simple. I've been deliberately repetitive because *that* is the key to habit formation: our brains like familiarity. (This is also why we will revisit this technique in Chapter Seven.) Now you get to decide which activity to apply this simple principle to, repeatedly.

You may want to have a crack at coming up with your own way of practising military grade mindfulness. Using the questions and statements in the exercise below as a guideline, choose an activity and write your plan on a piece of paper or in a notebook. Here is an example of mine:

Mindful swimming

Trigger

The last two lengths of every swim session.

Just do it

I will focus on seeing a split view every time I breathe (front crawl), so I should always be able to see under the water. I am focusing on this *one* aspect of swimming while every other aspect (breathing, arms, legs), will do what they've always done through muscle memory. I will notice the temptation to turn my head all the way out of the water and take panicky gulps of air. I will notice how each eye has a different view, one above the water line and one below. Any time I become distracted by my thoughts, I can congratulate myself for noticing and then bring my attention back to the split view.

Reward

I noticed how much better my head placement was and that I was more streamlined in the water. I felt calm and clear after swimming – I enjoyed the break from thinking and planning. This did not take any more time out of my day, and I feel great for exercising *and* practising mindfulness.

Lapses

Sometimes I talk myself out of going swimming, and this usually happens if I put off swimming until later in the day. First, I will congratulate myself for noticing this. Second, I will realise I am doing something which takes mental effort, which means I am growing and learning. Third, I will resolve to plan my swims in the morning and, if my boyfriend wants to sleep in, I'll leap out of bed and do my own thing rather than disappearing back under the duvet.

Exercise: Developing a military grade mindfulness HABIT

My plan:

- My new military grade mindfulness habit is...

- My trigger is...

- Any time I become distracted by thoughts, I will congratulate myself for noticing and then bring my attention back to...

After the activity:

- What did I notice that I normally wouldn't?

- How do I feel having taken a break from my frantic mind (while also training it at the same time)?

- How much extra time has it taken out of my day?

Lapses:

- Congratulate myself for noticing this in the first place. This is awareness and that is mindfulness.

- Remind myself that lapses are a sign of progress. Another pat on the back.

- What strategy could I try next time?

- How might I adapt one of the components to make it more effective?

Two years after I hit the wires in Morocco, I was flying down the Wye Valley, the part where England meets Wales. We had planned a tactical practice mission where we had to stay below the enemy radar and line of sight and 'attack' Tintern Abbey. On this occasion I was the navigator – think of the navigator's job as similar to that of a rally driver's co-pilot on a muddy forest track. Much like Morocco, the valley was steep-sided and winding, so the twists and turns came at us quickly. My role was to scour the map for sharp bends and obstructions (like wires) and to brief the pilot on what to expect. It was all going well. I had learned my lesson from Morocco. And then, bang! We hit wires. Again. This time though, I didn't start fantasising about my eulogy. There was no daydreaming about how I would die. I immediately sprang into action. I put out the mayday call, dropped the landing gear and prepared the aircraft for touch down on a fortuitously placed sandbank straight ahead. When we were safely down, I completed the shutdown drills and marked the spot on the GPS so we could pass the coordinates to rescue services. None of us were harmed. The aircraft was salvaged and fully repaired. Southeast Wales went without electricity for about two weeks (oops), but one mustn't cry over spilled milk.

A few days afterwards, the pilot approached me.

'Sarah, I just don't know how you did that. I was still processing what the fuck had happened, and by the time I worked it out you'd done everything. That was incredible. How did you do that?'

I remember shifting awkwardly and mumbling, 'Um, well, I have had some practice at this...' But that's the point. My brain already *knew* what to do. I had already trained my brain to respond in exactly the way it needed to under extreme pressure. I already knew where I needed to focus my attention. I'm not saying we need to crash helicopters to practise military grade mindfulness, of course (there are far cheaper and easier ways to do this), but the point is, we train and we train and we train so that when we need it most, our brain already knows what to do. It has become an automatic behaviour. Or even a Healthy Automatic Behaviour In Threatening Scenarios. A habit, in other words. If you take only one thing from this chapter, let it be this: 'Train hard, fight easy.' And don't ever get in a helicopter with me.

Applying HABITS

Here is a snazzy way to remember the techniques and tips that I've shared in the last two chapters using the HABIT mnemonic. I've also adapted it to be a handy aide-memoire for how to go about creating these healthy automatic behaviours:

H stands for Healthy: Remember to stay in the healthy part of the stress curve – ie eustress (or in *stretch*). This is where you do your best learning. A little bit of positive pressure is good for you; too little and you get lazy; too much and you start to sweat heavily, lose your shit and maybe cry.

A stands for Attention: You have probably created a learned behaviour of focusing your attention wherever your current activity dictates – ie you're not in the habit of focusing your attention where you choose. You need to commit to training your brain to focus attention in the one place you want it to be. Start today.

B stands for Be in one place: Not only can you focus your attention where you choose, you are infinitely better off when only one place has your focus. Work out what you need to do to make this easier for yourself by removing as many distractions as you can and communicating your intentions to others.

I stands for I: The biggest barrier to uni-tasking is other people, so try employing assertive but respectful communication strategies to protect your time. For example, 'I can see this is important to you, I'd like to give this my full attention. I could do that at X time. Would that suit you?'

T stands for 'Train hard, fight easy': Remember, you must train your brain to focus in one place during peacetime. This means practising uni-tasking when you feel calm and resourced, then you will have this healthy automatic behaviour to fall back on when you are in crisis.

S stands for Set the example: If you want everyone to leave you alone while you uni-task, then set the example. Do it first. I know this is hard. Nobody said being a trailblazer is easy, but you've got this. Go get 'em, tiger.

Key takeaways from Chapter Three

- We are not designed to be naturally cool under pressure.

- We revert to our learned and ingrained behaviours and thought patterns under stress.

- We can train our minds to ensure these behaviours are helpful – ie by repeatedly practising healthy habits.

- We perform and learn best when we are in 'stretch'.

- Mindfulness can help us to be less affected by stress and to recover more quickly from stress.

4

Play Hard, Fight Easy

Do you know someone whose life seems ridiculously easy? Everything they touch turns to gold? Here we are grinding away, overcoming challenges, confronting our weaknesses, working *so* hard to win at life, and yet there are others who seem to get a disproportionate share of good luck. Everything is easy. They don't appear to worry or need to worry about life. It's so bloody unfair. If we're honest (and this is a safe place to be honest), we feel like we're owed something that they are not. Because we toiled. We suffered. They didn't.

I hear you. In this chapter I'm going to look at how we can make training the mind not just effortless, but fun. Because let's face it, life is too bloody short to be miserable while we seek enlightenment. This isn't a pilgrimage; it's a goddamn party. You may have previously identified with phrases like:

- No pain, no gain.

- If it's too good to be true, it probably is.

- The harder the struggle, the more glorious the triumph.

In the military we were less profound and more masochistic. We used phrases like, 'If it's not raining, it's not training,' and, 'Practise bleeding'. While these remind us that learning and growing is not an easy path, that doesn't mean we have to be martyrs to the cause. We can have some fun while we learn.

The science bit

Extensive studies done on concert pianists, Olympic athletes and pilots (ie people who rely on their ability to keep cool and perform to an exceptional standard under stress) found conclusive results that these individuals were all less affected by stressful situations.[17] More accurately, when their stress response was activated, this group were able to 'switch on' the PNS and calm their threat system more quickly. They found that this ability could be measured by 'vagal' tone, since we use the vagus nerve to activate the PNS. They also discovered something exciting in the field of neurophysiology relative to the Heart Rate Variability (HRV).[18]

HRV is the measure of how regular our heartbeat is. We might think that a heart rate of 60bpm (beats per minute) means our hearts beat once every second, but in fact, the intervals between the heartbeats are not totally regular. This is good news. In fact, the more irregular the intervals, the

17   A Meland et al, 'Impact of mindfulness training on physiological measures of stress and objective measures of attention control in a military helicopter unit', *The International Journal of Aviation Psychology* (2015), https://doi.org/10.1080/10508414 .2015.1162639, accessed 26 May 2022

18   C Bergland, 'The psychology of flow and your vagus nerve', *Psychology Today* (2017), www.psychologytoday.com/gb/blog/the-athletes-way/201705/the-psychophysiology-flow-and-your-vagus-nerve, accessed 26 May 2022

higher the HRV; and the higher the HRV, the more likely we are to enjoy improved wellbeing, heart health, performance and, crucially, stress resilience. Clearly there is a huge benefit to increasing our HRV. So how do we do this? Let's go back to our group of concert pianists, Olympic athletes and pilots. Remember I said they had ninja levels of vagal tone? There is a way to exercise the vagus nerve to increase vagal tone. We do so by being blissfully and fully absorbed in optimally challenging activities (which are also known as flow).[19] Here are the characteristics of a flow activity:

- It's optimally challenging – ie it's on the sweet spot, or 'stretch' on the Yerkes-Dodson curve (illustrated in Chapter Two).

- It occupies our full attention.

- It's enjoyable.

Think of an occasion when you lost all sense of time because you were so absorbed by something you found enjoyable. It could have been building a kit car, or gardening, or crafting a kick-ass presentation for work. When you're this absorbed you are in flow, which means that flow is more accessible than you think. It isn't reserved for concert pianists. They just happened to provide us with the evidence. Being in the flow increases your vagal tone, which increases your HRV, which in turn

---

19   C Peifer et al, 'The relation of flow-experience and physiological arousal under stress – Can U shape it?', *Journal of Experimental Social Psychology* (July 2014), www.researchgate.net/publication/260044107_The_Relation_of_Flow-Experience_and_Physiological_Arousal_Under_Stress_-_Can_U_Shape_It, accessed 26 May 2022

increases your autonomic nervous system regulation (the SNS and the PNS), which then increases your stress resilience. And stress resilience is the backbone of military grade mindfulness.

What the discovery of flow has done is to illustrate that we can practise military grade mindfulness *while* we are doing the things we love, every day. Let's start thinking about things you love doing. Here are mine:

- Wine tasting

- Running

- Hanging out with my son (feeling slightly bad for not listing this one first)

For extra benefits in training, include the things you love doing that are optimally challenging. Here are mine:

- Flying helicopters

- Swimming

- Public speaking

The point is, these are all things you can do while practising military grade mindfulness, simply because you will be absorbed in what you're doing and are therefore exercising the vagus nerve.

 Take a moment to list the things you love which can help you execise your vagus nerve.

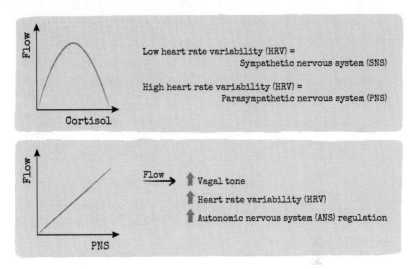

Relationship between flow and the autonomic nervous system

As we've said before, we *do* need to train, train, train, but there's no law that says training can't be fun. We 'train hard, fight easy', but we can also 'play hard, fight easy'.

Other reasons to play hard, fight easy

You may recall that we can activate our PNS, or deactivate our stress response, by slowing down our breathing, and because our thoughts, feelings and physical actions are all linked, just like magic, we will start to feel better. For the same reason, we can also alter other aspects of the cognitive framework and achieve the same effect. In other words, we can look at the hormones released and work out how to influence them.

When the SNS is activated, the body releases cortisol and adrenaline so that we can be super-alert and run away or turn and fight. When the PNS is activated, three feel-good hormones are released: endorphins (commonly associated with the high we get from exercise or eating chocolate), serotonin (usually associated with fresh air and sunlight) and oxytocin (known as the love hormone which is produced when we enjoy connection or physical intimacy). These feel-good hormones have the advantage of counteracting our cortisol levels, so if we increase these 'good' hormone levels, we can effectively reduce our overall stress.

The other advantage of lowering our cortisol levels is that it gives us more capacity to deal with the shit life throws at us on a day-to-day basis. Think about it like a wellbeing bank. The more deposits of 'good' hormones we put in, the more we have available to withdraw when we really need it. In other words, taking care of the basics from day to day goes a long way to keeping us resilient. Here are some of the everyday activities that will increase our 'good' hormones:

- Exercise

- Music

- Dance

- Eating nutritious food

- Fresh air

- Sex

- Random acts of kindness

- Yoga and meditation

- Play

What's even better is that many of these activities have multiple benefits. For example, nutritious food and exercise do wonders for our physical health as well as topping up the wellbeing bank. Play is another great example of this. There are several scientific sources which back up the benefits of 'play'.[20] These include increased creativity, problem-solving and emotional intelligence. Further, if we undertake play activities with others, it can also strengthen relationships and build rapport. My favourite version of this is to build Lego with my son. I find it to be a naturally mindful activity that I can become fully absorbed in, while my son absolutely loves the one-on-one time. Lego has also come to the rescue in our house when there has been a fractious atmosphere.

 Take a moment to write down some daily activities that you could do to increase the reserves in your wellbeing bank.

Remember, you can also practise mindfulness while doing these activities by simply choosing where to focus your attention while you do them. If you add mindfulness to these activities, you will be getting a threefold return because you will be increasing the reserves in the wellbeing bank, increasing your physical health and training your mind. One way to achieve all three benefits, for example, would be to adapt the mindful walking exercise during your daily run or cycle, taking turns to tune into each of your five senses. When you notice you

20   J Popović, 'The importance of play for enhancing the creativity', *Medium.com* (Aug 2017), https://medium.com/@janja.popovic/the-importance-of-play-for-enhancing-the-creativity-fbf69021593, accessed 26 May 2022

have become distracted, you can gently escort your attention back to where you want it to be. Think of mindfulness as a dance between two states: focusing and noticing. You are either *focusing* your attention where you want it to be or *noticing* where your attention is. Try telling me that you can't practise that literally anywhere and anytime – including during 'play'.

Try having fun

Let's go back to those annoying people that seem to find life easy. Why does that happen? Why should they be 'rewarded' when they've apparently put so little effort into being the best version of themselves or to overcoming difficulty? Well, first, these people *rarely* wear their struggles on their sleeve. Let's ignore the social media trend of, 'I've got it worse than you' for a moment – in my experience, everyone has something going in their life (or their heads) that they don't put on show. Every human feels pain and fear, it's just that we don't always shout about it. So it's usually a good idea to suspend judgement on someone else's 'fairy-tale' existence because the truth is, it's probably just as fucked up as yours. We will look at this in more detail in Chapter Six.

With all that said, there *is* evidence that some people find life 'easier', and it's because they, whether by luck or judgement, practise something which is now commonly referred to as 'positive psychology'. The origins of positive psychology are simple. Rather than trying to figure out how to get people with poor mental health back to the 'norm', the founders of this approach decided to study people who had unusually good mental health and tried to figure out why they were so happy – and if we could copy them.[21] Positive psychology is the antidote to the over-therapised and overly diagnostic culture that we live in. For too long, the emphasis has been on finding out what is wrong with someone, and in the case of therapy, understanding why and trying to figure out how to fix it. The problem with this method is that we are always looking for the worst, and if we look for it, we usually find it.

My theory of the truth is this: we are all a little bit fucked up. But that doesn't mean we are broken. What's more, I think we can, and should, learn to use these marvellous and fucked-up brains of ours to experience more joy and happiness. When we are having a good time, it's hard to remember to feel sorry for ourselves, or be pissed off at others for having it better than us, or worry about how inadequate we are. In essence, I'm suggesting you have a bit more fun. You may be surprised how your problems start to melt away.

This idea complements what we know about mindfulness and, in particular, military grade mindfulness. A study was conducted by Alison Carter called 'Mindfulness in the Military', which revealed, among many fascinating findings, that delving deep into the Pandora's box of our past can be counterproductive and actually *increase* trauma.[22] This is why I would always advise using a qualified therapist if you want to go back to your childhood and examine why you're so messed

21   R Al Taher, 'The 5 founding fathers and a history of positive psychology', *Positive Psychology.com* (February 2015), https://positivepsychology.com/founding-fathers, accessed 26 May 2022
22   A Carter and J Tobias Mortlock, 'Mindfulness in the military: improving mental fitness in the UK Armed Forces using next generation team mindfulness training', *IES* (2019), www.employment-studies.co.uk/system/files/resources/files/IES_MoD_mindfulness_report-525.pdf, accessed 26 May 2022

up. It is dangerous territory and one that should be navigated with care.

But what if we don't need to go back there at all? What if it's enough to acknowledge that we all have insecurities and challenges, and rather than devoting our energy to digging up these insecurities and challenges, we focus on the things that make us smile. If we're successful, those issues won't seem as important anymore. We don't need to unravel our pasts or revisit and ignite our disappointments. We can simply accept the situation for what it is, and then get on with enjoying life. What an exciting possibility.

The science certainly backs it up. When the experts studied unusually 'well' people, they found that not only did they spend their time doing meaningful things that made them happy, they were also more successful in their personal and professional lives. These mentally 'well' people believed good things would happen to them… and they did.[23] Much has been written about achieving happiness, one of the most popular books on the topic is probably *The Secret* by Rhonda Byrne.[24] Based on the principle of the law of attraction, the book's message is that if we expect good things to happen, we will create the conditions for these good things. We will also be more open to them happening, and thus more likely to benefit when they do happen. In other words, good things happen because they *can* happen. Conversely, the reason that good things don't happen to us is because we don't let them happen.

---

23   A Cope, *Flourishing in the Workplace: An investigation into the intentional strategies employed by those experiencing long-term positive affect in the UK public sector* [doctoral thesis] (2017), www.artofbrilliance.co.uk/Dr-Andy-Cope-Thesis.pdf, accessed 25 July 2022
24   R Byrne, *The Secret* (Simon and Schuster, 2006)

In summary, please take this as an invitation to have some fun. It is unlikely to do any harm (and may even do you immeasurable good). Here is an exercise you can try which embodies this sense of fun.

Exercise: Mindful drinking (or 'winefulness')

- Pour yourself a glass of your preferred beverage. My favourite is wine, but this works equally well with beer or nonalcoholic drinks such as tea or even water. Take a moment to notice how it looks in the glass. How does the light reflect off it? How does it move when you tilt the glass? If you notice you've started thinking about work/the future/the past, you can just smile at this point ('Aah, there goes my wonderful, busy brain again...') and then bring your attention back to your drink.

- Now smell it. What do you notice? How does your nose and mouth respond? If you are making judgements about what the liquid will taste like, or perhaps those thoughts about work have returned again, smile and then bring your attention back to your beverage.

- Now drink it. See if you can notice every tiny drop in your mouth. How it feels as you taste it. How your body responds. Become aware of any tendency to immediately have another sip. Did you get distracted by thoughts at any point? Worrying about the future? Planning? Ruminating over a past conversation? Overthinking? That's fine. That's what brains do. No need to beat yourself up over it. Just notice it, and then when you're ready, let that thought go and bring your attention back to your drink.

- Repeat.

Congratulations. You've just done my favourite meditation. In conclusion, if we want to rewire our brains, we need to commit to training, and training, and then training some more. But we can also play, play, and then play some more. Play hard, fight easy.

Key takeaways from Chapter Four

- The key to achieving better performance is to train, train, train, but there is no reason why this training can't be fun.

- Flow is a great way to train the mind while doing something enjoyable.

- We don't have to dig up painful thoughts and try and deal with them to improve our wellbeing. We can simply learn to focus our attention somewhere that nourishes us.

5

Learning To Sit
With Difficulty

I once had the privilege to meet an intriguing woman called Janet. She was a successful managing director of an engineering firm. She had a good salary, plenty of friends and took nice holidays. The most striking thing about her was her effortless confidence. She appeared invincible. A born leader. She was bright, vivacious and funny. I was quite intimidated by her and if I'm honest, I wanted to dislike her. But when she told me her story, I quickly realised this was a wounded soul who desperately wanted to be free from her pain. She had been in therapy for years which, it seemed, had only made things worse. When she told me her story, I had to work hard to keep my jaw from falling to the ground.

Janet's story

Janet was blissfully and happily married. It wasn't the normal, 'comfortably contented but a bit dull' kind of marriage. She and her husband were outrageously in love. They were both successful and driven and had been through a tough couple of years when they'd travelled a lot for their jobs. They were the cliched 'ships in the night', but recognising this was an issue, they had both found a way to reposition within their companies so that they could be together every day. It was like something from a fairy tale. 'I just couldn't believe how lucky I was to have found this man I utterly adored and who utterly adored me back,' Janet told me. 'We were physically, spiritually, intellectually and emotionally soulmates. And our life had just become perfect.'

To celebrate this new chapter in their life they booked a holiday to New Zealand – a place that had always been on their bucket list. Ten days before they were due to fly out, Janet woke up in a hospital bed with a neck brace on. She didn't know why she was there, but the presence of a police officer by her bed indicated it was something serious. The police officer informed Janet that her husband had tried to murder her in her sleep and had then taken an overdose. Paramedics had resuscitated them both. Janet recalled there was something off in the way the police questioned her. They kept asking questions like, 'How long has your husband been abusive?' None of it made sense and she felt she was being coerced into saying something that wasn't true, so she said nothing. She was completely and utterly disorientated. She'd gone from planning holiday outfits with the man of her dreams, to being told he had tried to murder her.

Over the next few days, Janet's memory returned, and she was able to recall her husband standing over the bed in a trancelike state. She remembered his hands around her neck and then she'd quickly fallen unconscious. Her husband was charged with attempted murder, a prosecution that Janet did not support, so she stood by him for the several months it took for the case to be heard in court. He was eventually acquitted. The court ruled that the incident had been a tragic accident. The judge believed Janet's husband had suffered an 'out-of-body experience', and he now felt deep remorse and shame for what he had done. The judge further observed that this 'episode' had been born out of repressed mental health issues that Janet's husband hadn't even been aware were present. The traumatic event would have been almost impossible to predict, and luckily, he had regained his senses before Janet was more seriously, or even fatally, injured.

The judge urged the court to take this case as a sobering reminder that people can do unthinkable things when they are at breaking point and that we each have a responsibility to take care of our mental health, not only for ourselves, but also for those around us. Janet and her husband were finally able to move on with their lives and took steps to prevent anything like that from ever happening again. Janet had learned a sobering lesson. She learned that people (even those closest to you) who appear to be strong and happy can be drowning underneath. She had learned that it was possible for the man who loved her to hurt her, and she had learned that good people do bad things.

Why Janet couldn't move on

As the years passed, Janet struggled to put it behind her. She couldn't seem to let go of the pain and darkness that never seemed to leave her. She had a knot in her chest that wouldn't go away. It didn't particularly surprise her. What had happened was traumatic and Janet knew it would take time to heal. As part of the healing process, Janet painfully evaluated all her feelings and emotions, and was surprised to discover that the action, what her husband had done to her, was not what was holding her back. What she was struggling with was the way the world had responded when she'd been in the greatest pain of her life. This was the reason that she'd sought my help.

Janet explained that some people had tried to shift the blame her way, citing her tricky character. 'It sounds mad,' she told me, 'but I can understand that people must have wondered what on earth I had done to bring him to such lows – he was such a genuine, nice guy, always had time for people, one of life's lovelies. People were searching for explanations as to how he could do something like this, and I'm not surprised they arrived at me.' Others, she said, reached out initially, and then went silent. When she bumped into them, they would vaguely enquire, 'So what happened? Did it all go away?'

Many felt sorry and worried for her husband. At the time of the attack, it transpired, he had been in a deep depression triggered by a traumatic incident at work. After his assault on Janet, her husband had been suicidal for many months afterwards and had believed he was going to jail for a crime he had not committed. Though he had attacked her, he had never intended to cause her harm. In the agonising months while they waited for the trial, many would approach Janet and ask how her husband was managing. Janet told me, 'I'm sure they would have asked me how I was too; it's the British way. But I've erased that part from my memory. I realised within a few days of the accident that people were more worried about my husband than they were about me. After all, I was back at work, and I was "fine". It almost felt like people had forgotten that I had been affected too. I found myself wanting to remind them, even embellish it a bit just so I could get them to see I'd been hurt in this, too. I couldn't quite get over how the world had moved on so quickly while I was processing the worst pain of my life.'

I asked Janet to describe how this had affected her. She responded without hesitation. 'Invisible,' she said. 'I felt invisible.' Janet was in a lot of pain and needed a witness for that pain. She needed to feel like her pain meant something to the world, that it was more than just a flicker of interest in someone's social media feed. She needed an empathetic witness in a world where empathy appeared scarce. Janet started to take this personally, asking herself why she had provoked people to respond so heartlessly. In a perverse kind of way, Janet was taking too much credit for other people's behaviours. She was terrified that she had *made* people respond the way they had and that she must be a monster.

Janet found this thought so unbearable that she had tried to correct it by finding other ways to make sense of it. She became obsessed with trying to explain other people's behaviour so she could deflect some of the blame away from herself. If she could make other people into monsters, then maybe she wasn't a monster herself, but that didn't help, because that left her living in a monstrous world. Next, Janet tried to reason that other people mustn't have realised she was drowning. 'I appeared so strong, even scary, to the outside world,' she repeatedly told me. Round and round she went, trying to guess what other people were thinking and trying to understand why they had forsaken her.

The result was that Janet felt like a failure for not being able to work through her issues and for being misunderstood by the rest of the world. She was stuck in a constant internal battle, leaving her angry and hurt. She was also extremely sad. The tragedy was that in trying so hard to eliminate her pain, she had ended up magnifying it. She had created a world full of monsters to make sense of her pain.

Janet's story is a great example of one of the main reasons why I don't use cognitive behavioural therapy (CBT) – or rather, that I use it with caution. The main principle behind CBT is that our thoughts govern how we feel and behave, and that these thoughts are often wrong. They are referred to as 'thinking errors', so if we can change how we think, we can change how we feel.

Why it's difficult to change our thoughts

Janet had tried to do this. She had tried to replace hateful and paranoid thoughts with more rational ones, but she was spending a lot of time trying to guess what was motivating other people's behaviour. She was trying to mind-read, which is basically a pointless exercise. Janet wound up feeling like a failure, because she couldn't change her thoughts around what other people were thinking. She was also telling herself that she must be taking things the wrong way and that she was wrong to feel hurt, which reduced her self-esteem even further. She became convinced that there was a fundamental limitation in the way her brain made sense of things, and that is exactly the problem. In trying to correct her thoughts, Janet had ended up in an increasingly miserable and angry battle with herself.

I am not saying our thoughts are always right or helpful, but in my experience, trying to simply change them just invites further thought and further conflict. As Andy Puddicombe from Headspace says, 'Thinking about a problem is still thinking... which is often the problem.'[25] Certainly, this was the case for Janet. Janet didn't need to change her thoughts. What she'd been through had been awful, and in all likelihood some people had let her down. There was nothing wrong with her for finding that painful, and there was no need for her to focus on correcting her thoughts about the incident. What she needed to do was change her *relationship* with her thoughts. She needed to learn to sit with them without fighting them or inflaming them. She needed to learn to sit with her pain. That way, she wouldn't need the world to be her empathetic witness. She would become her own empathetic witness. She needed to learn 'distress tolerance'.

Janet resisted my suggestion initially. 'Isn't that just the same as throwing a self-pity party? Aren't I just dwelling on unhelpful thoughts and further tormenting myself?' And this is a germane point, but distress tolerance is not about dwelling on thoughts. It's about witnessing them. There is a subtle, but important, difference and it takes practice. I refer to this as A-level mindfulness, and there is a reason why I am covering this in Chapter Five and not Chapter One. Practising distress tolerance requires a firm foundation of mindfulness techniques so that we can do it without causing further trauma. More on that later. First, it's important to understand why we would put ourselves through this process in the first place.

---

25   'Andy Puddicombe' (Headspace, no date),
www.headspace.com/andy-puddicombe, accessed 9 June 2022

Why do we feel pain?

To understand why distress tolerance is so important, we need to begin by examining why we feel pain and why we resist it. We experience pain for the simple reason that it keeps us alive. If we didn't experience pain, we could do lasting damage to ourselves. Pain tells us to rest when we are injured. It tells us to take our hand off a burning stove and it's our bodies' way of telling us to stop doing something and avoid doing it in the future. Once we've touched a hot stove, for example, we are likely to be more cautious next time round, hence the phrase, 'Once bitten, twice shy.'

Pain has a distinct survival advantage. Pain can be mental as well as physical, and it serves the same purpose. They once conducted 'Cyberball' experiments where people were assigned avatars and participated in a virtual ball-tossing game.[26] Partway into the game, one person out of a group of three would be deliberately excluded from the game by not having the ball tossed to them any longer. FMRI (functional magnetic resonance imaging measures brain activity by detecting changes associated with blood flow) revealed that the part of the brain responsible for the 'suffering component of pain' was highly active in the individuals when they were left out. Further, the five different regions of the brain that trigger physical pain also lit up during this study. The brain was registering that rejection as painful, even though it wasn't physical, which explains why we feel heartache when going through a break-up.

---

26   D Rock, 'Status: A more accurate way of understanding self-esteem', *Psychology Today* (October 2009), www.psychologytoday.com/gb/blog/your-brain-work/200910/status-more-accurate-way-understanding-self-esteem, accessed 26 May 2022

Though this pain is not much fun, it's rooted in our evolution because it relates to our need to be part of a troop, presumably because there is safety in numbers. We are wired to stay within a herd and rejection is tantamount to death. We will sometimes go to extraordinary lengths to avoid this pain and ensure we stay in the herd, and thus, stay alive. What we need to understand then, is that our pain is trying to help us. It's trying to signal danger. We also need to understand that we're hardwired to resist pain and to do whatever it takes to remove the cause of the pain and get out of danger. In the twenty-first century though, because we are no longer risking our lives daily (eg hunting, gathering food), this desire to resist and remove pain can lead to all sorts of problems. Examples include avoidance behaviour (eg staying single in the hope of avoiding heartache), unhelpful coping strategies (eg excessive drinking) or, in Janet's case, a strong desire to rewrite history so she could erase the source of the pain. Although understandable and entirely instinctive, resisting pain can often make the problem worse.

Emotions have positive intentions

When pain manifests in the form of unpleasant emotions, it could be signalling a number of 'harsh-but-true' lessons that we can use to promote positive action. Let's look at a few examples:

- **Sadness:** This can signal to us that we are missing something in our lives and, when we stop to listen to it, we might begin to appreciate what that is. It could be a better option than burying our sadness in a fog of Chardonnay, loud music and outrageous feathered hats (hypothetically speaking, you understand). Maybe we have lost our sense of closeness with a family member, and this could be the impetus we need to take that first brave step, swallow our pride, and apologise for being so ungrateful about the ghastly centrepiece they insisted on buying us for our dinner table.

- **Anger:** This can signal that we feel wronged in some way and can be the fuel we need to have that long overdue, awkward conversation and stand up for our beliefs and values.

- **Anxiety:** This can tell us we feel under-resourced to deal with certain work demands and could nudge us towards asking for more help or time with a project, or saying no to extra demands every now and then (radical, I know).

In Janet's case, her anger was telling her that she had been wronged. Her fear was preventing her from seeing this because she was terrified that somehow, she deserved what had befallen her. Once Janet gave herself permission to sit with both her anger and her fear, she realised that what she needed to do was grieve. She needed to grieve the fact that a younger, naiver version of herself had died on the day her husband attacked her. She needed to grieve for the loss of her innocence. She needed to grieve for the girl who believed the whole world would come running to her side when she was in pain, and she needed to grieve for the 'perfect life' she felt she had lost in that awful split-second moment.

Janet practised a series of 'sitting with difficulty' meditations for a week. She cried for a week. And then she came back to me and said, 'I realise now I was not broken. I was broken-hearted. It sounds weird, but when I saw myself in this way, I saw that behind the tigress exterior was a frightened, lonely girl and I just wanted to put my arms around her. It was the first time I can remember not hating myself.' When Janet released herself from the need to fix things and instead just acknowledged the utter shittiness of what happened, she was able to do something that had hitherto proved elusive. She was able to heal. In other words, cultivating an ability to sit with and tolerate her pain was the key to diminishing it. There is also a beautiful simplicity here. Rather than having to do something about our thoughts and feelings, we can simply observe them, *and sometimes that's enough.*

Empathy triumphs over reason

So why is it that simply observing our thoughts is enough? For the same reason that parenting books tell us we should start with empathy and then redirect with logic. When our child cries because they lose their favourite toy, our instinctive response might be to say, 'Don't cry,' because:

- We know it's not the end of the world so doesn't justify the sudden outburst.

- We don't like seeing our child in pain and we want to reduce their pain by encouraging some perspective.

- It's really embarrassing when your toddler has a meltdown in the middle of the supermarket.

But here's what's really happening when you tell a child not to cry:

- You are telling them their feelings aren't valid, which means they will eventually learn to distrust their feelings or hate themselves for having emotions.

- You are telling them their thoughts are wrong because they've given too much meaning to a teddy bear.

- You are asking someone else to change their behaviour to reduce your own discomfort.

What a minefield. The textbook response is to say, 'I can see that teddy was important to you. You must be feeling really sad.' Then pause. This way you are letting them know you will sit with them through their difficulty, that their pain is important to you, and that you will acknowledge it. Then, when that emotion has diminished (because it will – see next paragraph), you can insert some logic or redirect their attention away from the source of the pain. For example, 'How could we make the situation better? Shall we have a look for teddy together?' Even though this book is not about parenting skills, there are some salient lessons to be learned from this technique. We all have an inner child, and we can learn a lot from understanding it.

Bringing it back to the adult world, think about when you are wound up by something and you vent to your friend or partner. You got overlooked for a promotion that you have worked your butt off for, putting in the extra hours, missing birthday parties, dazzling your boss with your well-researched and dizzying intellect, painstakingly going the extra mile to produce consistently excellent results. You know you are the best person for the job, and you've stopped at nothing to prove your worth. And then the promotion goes to the office clown who the boss happens to play golf with…

When you get home, you walk through the door and relay this story to your partner. Do you want your partner to pour you a large glass of wine, sit you down and say, 'My God, that is just utterly rubbish and you didn't deserve that,' or say, 'Well, I guess all that effort wasn't really worth it then,' and go back to playing sudoku? If my partner tried the second response on me, he'd get a four-letter word response. Though the second response is a rational conclusion to draw from the situation, it is most likely not what you need at that precise moment. In that moment, you want your partner to feel your pain. You want to know that your suffering means something to someone. What you don't want is a briefly thought-through solution that undermines your pain or makes you feel stupid or sidelined.

Empathy is not a soft skill

Arthur Labinjo-Hughes died at the age of six years old from brain injuries.[27] He had been abused, starved and poisoned by his father and stepmother for a protracted period before he died. He had experienced unimaginable and horrific suffering. When the article hit the papers my own son, who shares the same name, was also six years old. It hit me hard. The grief I felt when I saw the image of the innocent, smiling boy who

27   J Murray, 'Arthur Labinjo-Hughes: Timeline of events that ended in his murder', *Guardian* (December 2021), www.theguardian.com/society/2021/dec/03/arthur-labinjo-hughes-timeline-of-events-that-ended-in-his, accessed 26 May 2022

had been tortured by his parents was like a punch in the solar plexus. I could physically feel my throat constricting and a sharp pain in my chest, such was my repulsion for what I was reading. My instinctive reaction was to turn away from this pain, followed by a natural urge to reduce what I did feel. I didn't want to read the article. 'At least he isn't suffering now,' I remember thinking as a weak consolation.

The example I am using is shocking and awful, but I am using it on purpose. The thought of a little boy suffering is utterly appalling, but I decided to overcome the urge to turn away from it, and instead chose to sit in meditation. I wanted to be an empathetic witness to this little boy's pain in the full knowledge that I was utterly powerless to change his past or do anything to help him. I didn't want to do this because it made me feel better or because it would help him in any way, but because I wanted to show that respect to him by acknowledging his pain. I think that acknowledging someone else's pain, feeling pain for them, is the highest compliment you can pay another human, even though it won't make their pain go away.

Empathy is sometimes seen as feminine and therefore a 'soft' trait in female leaders, but showing empathy to ourselves and others is genuinely hard. It requires us to acknowledge uncomfortable truths and unpleasant emotions. Showing empathy requires courage.

Empathy makes the world better

Let's recap. Empathy allows us to acknowledge our pain, which will often then diminish of its own accord, so empathy is basically magic. It's a ninja skill that is neither easy nor instinctive, and because of that, it's the highest compliment you can pay to another human. But there's more. Empathy allows us to learn and grow. It allows us to recall some of the reasons we feel pain in the first place. If we avoid pain, then we are potentially denying ourselves powerful insight.

The articles around Arthur Labinjo-Hughes cited various 'missed opportunities' by social workers and police to spot the signs and intervene. Some defences were made and it's understandable. I can't imagine there is a single human who would want to bear the pain of knowing they could have helped that little boy but didn't. It is far less painful if they can convince themselves there is nothing they could have done. And maybe they're right. But what if they're not? You see, if those people don't have the ability to bear that pain, someone else's pain, they need to find an excuse. They need to insist on being powerless. But if they can acknowledge the true awfulness of what happened and the horrific possibility that they could have done more, if they can sit with that pain, they can learn from it. Sitting with difficulty is not only a valuable life skill, it also gives us the courage to learn from truly awful situations and, as in this context, may even save lives. Become your own empathetic witness, and the world will not only be a better place for you, but it will be a better place because of you.

Managing distress tolerance

I mentioned before that sitting with pain – ie distress tolerance – is a ninja skill. And it is. Acknowledging difficult emotions is useful for the precise reason that it gives us the power to tolerate pain rather than being at the mercy of it. We don't *have* to do anything daft or damaging in response to pain because we *can* just sit with the pain. Janet was so busy trying to reduce her pain that she was doing herself more damage. She had skipped out the acceptance part and wasn't giving herself permission to validate her own feelings. Taking time to acknowledge the shittiness of something is a helpful, and sometimes necessary, precondition for being able to let go and move on.

There is an easy way to keep the balance right with distress tolerance. Make it time-bound. Give yourself time and permission to practise distress tolerance and then move on to something that you can influence and that serves your needs and values – ie notice your pain for a specified amount of time and then focus on something else. Just because we *can* sit with pain doesn't mean we should make a time-consuming habit out of it. Cultivating an ability to sit with pain is helpful. Cultivating an addiction to sitting with pain is not. Keep this in mind when you practise the exercises below. They are a means to an end, not an end in themselves.

Exercise: Staring game

- Find a willing partner and then set a timer for two minutes.
- Stare deeply into your partner's eyes.
- You are not allowed to talk or laugh or do anything that will ease your discomfort. (You'll probably feel intensely uncomfortable quickly.)
- Sit with that discomfort until the timer rings.

The object of this exercise is to help you realise that dis-comfort is tolerable.

(Disclaimer: Not recommended on busy trains with un-initiated fellow passengers.)

Exercise: Waiting in queues

- The next time you're standing in a queue, held up at traffic lights or stuck behind a slow driver when you're late for a meeting, use this as a trigger to practise distress tolerance.

- Tolerate the frustration without the need to huff and puff, to tailgate, to rev your engine or tap your foot impatiently.

- If you find this helpful, say to yourself, 'I'm practising distress tolerance. I'm going on a mental gym session.' You are tolerating discomfort.

Exercise: Noticing the anger

I like to practise this exercise when I'm feeling angry, but it can be used for any unpleasant emotion.

- Set your timer for thirty seconds.

- Allow yourself to be curious about your anger. Where do you feel it in your body? Does it feel hot? Does it have a colour? Is it loud?

- Allow your anger to manifest in your body wherever it wants to. You don't need to act on it. You don't need to shout or stomp. You can just witness how it feels.

- After thirty seconds, make five long exhales, releasing the anger from every part of your body.

Everything passes, even pain

Often, the best way to deal with strong emotions is to witness them without trying to change them. When our emotions are validated with empathy, something magic happens. They kind of, well, calm down. We feel heard, so we don't have to shout anymore. That's it. It really is that simple. Because thoughts and feelings, no matter how urgent and overwhelming they feel in the moment, don't last forever. They are transient. They fade away. Of course, they may return, but they will again recede, like the eternal ebb and flow of a tidal river that slowly makes its way out to sea.

When we understand that feelings are transient, we realise that if we sit still for long enough without doing anything clever or special, these feelings will take care of themselves. Our pain will diminish, and in fact, for all the reasons above, it will diminish quicker when we give it an empathetic audience. I know it may sound counterintuitive to sit with pain, but accepting and acknowledging pain is not the same as surrendering. It sounds woo-woo, but it's precisely the opposite, because if we do what comes naturally (which is to suppress or inflame those thoughts and feelings), we just wind up feeling miserable for longer. This is why becoming our own empathetic witness can be so empowering. We now have the ability to bear witness to our own pain in a compassionate way and allow it to fade away without fighting it.

Extra bonus: You won't have to dump your partner for consistently choosing the second option – you'll always have your own option available to you. Recall that Janet so desperately wanted the world to witness her pain, and yet it appeared not to. Sadly, this is kind of the world we live in. The truth is, no matter how much shit you are going through, other people are going through their own shit too. It's not that your pain isn't important; it's that most of the time other people are doing their best to keep their heads above water and not be buried by their own grief. If we think about it, since we are programmed to resist pain, people are hardly going to be queueing up to bear *our* pain as well as theirs. The sooner you can cultivate an ability to be your own empathetic witness, the sooner you can release yourself, and others, of the burden of co-dependency. The meditation below may help you as you learn to sit with difficulty.

Meditation: Sitting with difficulty

Read through the following instructions several times or listen to the guided meditation on Soundcloud at https://soundcloud.com/user-978445649 – 'Sitting with difficulty'.

- Begin your meditation with your feet on the floor, bottom on the chair, relaxed but intentional posture, and softly lowered gaze or closed eyes.

- When you're ready, bring your attention to your breath. Notice each breath in and each breath out. Don't try and change it, just simply observe your breath.

- If you notice your attention has wandered to painful thoughts or feelings, allow the sensations to be present in your body without resisting them.

- If nothing has come to mind, try to recall a situation that has been causing you difficulty. It doesn't have to be anything major – just enough for the difficulty to come to mind now.

- Check in with how this uncomfortable experience shows up for you. What physical sensation occurs with these thoughts or emotions? What reaction do you have to these sensations? Do you notice any tendency to engage with these emotions – analysing, problem-solving, brooding?

- Now imagine, if you can, observing yourself in this moment. You might like to visualise yourself wherever you are sitting now, as if witnessing this moment from an out-of-body experience.

- See if you can visualise just sitting next to the version of you that is in pain and just witnessing that pain. There is nothing to say and no need to try and give an opinion or to take the pain away. It is simply enough to sit in companionable silence, acknowledging your pain.

- If you like, you might say, 'It's OK to feel like this. Whatever it is, it is OK to feel like this.'

- Now see if you can notice where in your body you feel this pain the most. You can rest your attention there for a while.

- Imagine breathing into and nourishing that part of the body and then exhaling and letting go of any tension that is there.

- When you notice the bodily sensations are no longer pulling so strongly for your attention, return your focus to your breath, remembering that you always have this as an anchor.

- When you are ready, you can open your eyes.

Come back to this meditation as often as you need to. The more you can be comfortable sitting with your feelings, with compassion and kindness towards yourself, the less of a grip they tend to have on you.

Key takeaways from Chapter Five

- We often feel an urge to wrestle with, bury or fuel our painful thoughts and emotions, which can lead to more pain.

- We can train ourselves to sit with difficulty and to tolerate the emotion without trying to fight it.

- This can help us to accept painful experiences with kindness, be our own empathetic witness and, ultimately, to move on with our lives.

- Empathy is not a 'soft skill'. It requires courage and makes us acknowledge uncomfortable truths and unpleasant emotions.

- Distress tolerance is better practised in small doses and when it is time-bound – ie noticing your pain for a specified amount of time and then focusing on something else.

6

No One Is Coming

At this point in our journey, it will be helpful to recap what we talked about in Chapter One. We are hardwired to react, *not* to think. Which means not only are we giving away our choices, but we probably don't even realise we have them in the first place. (Yes, I just quoted myself again, but I'm keen for you to see the golden thread here, so please bear with.)

Why we sometimes adopt the victim mindset

Even when things are going well for us, our brains will default to giving our power away, so we need to make a deliberate effort to take charge of our brains to live a conscious and fulfilled life. One that does justice to our potential. We have to *learn* to take control of our lives; but a note of caution, what can be learned can also be unlearned, sadly.

In the seventies, Martin Seligman conducted extensive research to determine what happens to us when we are stripped of our sense of power.[28] In a series of experiments that I can only assume would be illegal in today's world, he put dogs in cages and administered random electric shocks. The only way for the dogs to avoid these shocks was to escape, which is exactly what they tried to do. That bit is not surprising when you remember we are programmed to resist pain. What *was* surprising about this experiment was what happened next. After just a few sets of treatments, the dogs gave up trying to escape. Even though they knew they would continue to receive the electric shock treatments, they lay down in their cages and simply waited to be tortured. They accepted their misery. Astonishing.

What Seligman had discovered was what he coined 'learned helplessness', more commonly referred to today as 'victim mindset' – ie the state when we believe we are incapable of changing the circumstances of our situation and blame everyone else for our misery. At the time, Seligman believed he had demonstrated that helplessness is a learned behaviour, but subsequent studies have revealed the opposite to be true. Our default is to assume we have no power and to give our choices away, which is why the brain operates on autopilot most of the time.[29] As we grow, we *learn* to exercise more autonomy and independence, so what Seligman's experiments in fact revealed was that certain conditions can cause us to regress to our natural state of choicelessness.

28   MEP Seligman. 'Learned helplessness', *Annual Review of Medicine*, 23 (1972), pp407–12, www.annualreviews.org/doi/abs/10.1146/annurev.me.23.020172.002203, accessed 9 June 2022
29   SF Maier and MEP Seligman, 'Learned helplessness at fifty: Insights from neuroscience', *Psychological Review*, 123/4 (2016), www.ncbi.nlm.nih.gov/pmc/articles/PMC4920136, accessed 9 June 2022

So, what are those conditions? The crucial bit here is that the dogs were in an environment where they had little or no choice, so they were reminded of their powerlessness. The other crucial part is that the experience was unpleasant. In summary: Distress + Powerlessness = Learned Helplessness.

Conditions during the Covid-19 pandemic provided the perfect example of this. Life changed immeasurably: social distancing, curfews, lockdowns, work-from-home guidance, etc, were the order of the day. In other words, there were lots of rules imposed on us which were designed to keep us safe but ultimately took our power away from us. Add to that the distress of being separated from loved ones, living in isolation, home-schooling, being alone with our thoughts during furlough, not knowing what to plan for Christmas, not knowing if we'd be forever stranded somewhere exotic should we have chosen to take a holiday (I can think of worse things, personally…), etc. Do you see what I see? The *perfect conditions* for learned helplessness. The perfect conditions for people to give up and accept their circumstances. The perfect conditions for our brains to revert to being on autopilot and give away our choices, perhaps without even realising it.

Studies in the UK workplace have shown that almost 60% of employees complain of feeling anxious and over 50% describe feeling low.[30] This is classic victim mindset, and it's everywhere. Victim mindset comes from an unconscious belief that we are not worthy or capable of improving our situation. The media doesn't help here either. The news is often full

30   H Bliss, 'Employee wellbeing statistics: UK 2022' (Champion Health, 2022), https://championhealth.co.uk/insights/employee-wellbeing-statistics, accessed 9 June 2022

of stories about how stress levels, depression and loneliness are on the rise, and the finger is almost always pointed at the government or large corporations and their leadership. We even see this victim mindset in the way that lawsuits and trials are reported. While our legal system may operate under an 'innocent until proven guilty' assumption, media reporting is often the opposite. Published narratives will often demonise the accused and run emotive stories about the victims, even if there are no hard facts to justify this. A blame culture teaches us to point the finger elsewhere. It is easy to assume our misery is someone else's problem. Indeed, it can be quite comforting to think this, because then we don't have to feel stupid for feeling so crap.

All of this may sound a little deflating, and perhaps even a bit soap-boxy, but I'm passionate about this because human beings are frickin' awesome. The potential of the human brain is literally unquantifiable, and yet we've convinced ourselves we are powerless. It's high time we rejected the powerless and fragile narrative. It's time to take our power back. I'm going to provide inspiration from one of the most appalling victim stories in living memory. (I promise it will start getting upbeat soon. Remember you *can* tolerate discomfort, so hang in there.)

Everyone has their own shit going on

In Victor Frankl's humbling memoir, *Man's Search for Meaning*,[31] he described his experience of concentration camps and how

---

31   V Frankl, *Man's Search for Meaning* (Rider, 2004)

he came to discover the secret for happiness. He wrote that during the first phase of incarceration, many would shield themselves from confronting the horror of the situation by being in denial. (We refer to that in the military as 'shock of capture'.) After that, apathy quickly set in. The prisoners reverted to simply surviving in an animalistic way and gave up on living. In other words, they accepted their fate, much like the dogs in cages.

When they were set free, those that made it struggled at first to accept their change in luck, but also to integrate with others. They felt, quite understandably, that they were owed compassion by the outside world, but tragically, that wasn't forthcoming. Those who hadn't experienced the camps would shrug their shoulders and remark how they too had suffered, using rationing as their comparator. This highlights a fundamental point that we must understand. There is no hierarchy to suffering. If you get hit by a car, lose your partner and then have your house burgled, you are not owed good luck for the rest of your life. What's more, the reality is that most people will carry on with their lives while you try to rebuild the car crash that yours has become. Remember, everyone is going through their own shit, and everyone thinks that their shit is the worst shit ever.

My most vivid personal example of this was when I was leading a detachment of pilots in Kabul. We had been given the nod that we might be required, on short notice, to do a hostage rescue mission. We were asked to be ready for a 6am start, so I briefed the crews and sent them to bed early. At about midnight, I had a call to say it was unlikely to happen before 10pm the following day, at which point my crews would have been on duty for sixteen hours.

Rather than disturb their sleep in the middle of the night, I decided to let the crews have a full night's rest and inform them of the update in the morning. When I briefed them the following day, I told them they could relax, and I would call them back into the operations room when they were needed. It wasn't an ideal solution, but it was the best I could think of at the time. Two of the crew were outraged by this decision. They complained bitterly about being asked to do such a long day. They 'couldn't possibly' go back to sleep during the day and argued that I was asking them to 'stag on'. I still find it hard to believe that some of the crew put their own minor discomfort ahead of that hostage, but they did. Remember, everyone is going through their own shit and everyone thinks that their shit is the worst shit ever. No matter how unfair life has been to you, you probably won't get a gold medal for enduring it. This may not be fair or right, but it is often how life is. It is not hard to see why victim mindset, once we are in its grip, is hard to escape. But there is a way out.

Owning your shit

Frankl revealed the secret that separated those who kept their sense of self and went on to be happy from those who accepted victimhood as their new identity and stayed miserable. Those who thrived found happiness by focusing on cherished memories or a nice conversation with their loved ones – even if it was only in their imagination. It was something the guards couldn't take away from them. They would turn their attention to the beautiful sunset or birdsong. Some even managed to focus their attention on the comedic potential of their experiences. They joked about what odd dinner party guests they would be when asking for the soup from the bottom of the bowl (where the few, nutritious peas were found). Some made deliberate and somewhat risky decisions to live defiantly in accordance with their values by, for example, showing compassion and giving bread to those who were weaker. It is a testament to the limitless strength of the human mind that these people could keep a tiny kernel of control when everything else had been stripped away from them. It serves as one of the most inspirational examples of human resilience in history, which we would do well to learn from. The lesson is this: as long as we keep exercising choices, we are more powerful than any malevolent force. They chose to cherish memories, they chose to look for beauty in nature, they chose to help other prisoners, and so they remained powerful against all the odds.

It's not just about exercising choices, however. Even though this is both liberating and empowering, there is something else which distinguishes the victors from the victims. When we suffer, the victim's instinct is to try and justify this suffering by finding some meaning. 'Everything happens for a reason' is often used to try to offset emotional pain, but the danger here is that we become so obsessed with trying to find meaning in our suffering that we forget to actually grow from the experience and instead become defined by it. We go down the over-therapised route of looking for a reason to justify how damaged we are in the mistaken belief that we will feel better for it, but in reality, we are just limiting ourselves to being martyrs forever and we stay stuck with our pain. Frankl understood this insatiable drive for meaning, but he also understood that it is the *responsibility* that we feel towards our choices that determines our meaning. Nobody can get into our heads and think for us. Nobody can make us feel something. Simple test: when someone says, 'Cheer up,' when you are sad, do you suddenly and inexplicably feel cheerful, or do you want to staple things to their forehead? Nobody can tell us what meaning to give to our experiences. Nobody can make those choices for us, that power is ours and ours alone and therefore that responsibility is ours. Victors understand this. Victors own their shit. We can play this out through the simple exercise below.

Exercise: Owning your shit

Draw two circles, one inside the other. The one on the outside is the 'circle of concern' and the one on the inside is the 'circle of influence'.

First write down all the things you are concerned about, but cannot control or change, in the outer circle. Good examples of these are:

- Weather
- Politicians
- The media
- The past
- What other people think and say (ie other people being dicks)

Now write down all the things you care about and can influence in the inner circle. Here are some correlating examples:

- Book a holiday/move somewhere sunny
- Remember to vote

- Limit your exposure to the news

- Let the past go and concentrate on building your best future

- Be the best person you can be (ie don't be a dick)

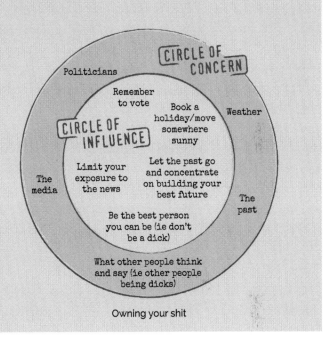

We spend a lot of time worrying about things we can't change – which is a pointless waste of energy and convinces us that we're powerless. Worrying about our circle of concern (outer circle) is a classic victim mindset thing to do. Not only that, but the more we worry about our outer circle of concern, the bigger it gets, so we actually convince ourselves we are more powerless than we really are. What we *should* be doing to better serve ourselves is to focus our attention on the inner circle, our circle of influence.

Taking back your power

What can you do? Even if it's only 10% of the solution, it's 10% that you have influence over. Writing this stuff down can remind you that you often have more agency over things than you think. In the above diagram, for example, you may have no control over the weather, yet arguably, you could reduce your carbon footprint and that activity may, in time, have some influence over the climate and weather. This thought process helps you to become choice aware. It helps you to feel powerful and it also helps you to get shit done. It's a win-win scenario. Once you've decided what is in which circle, you can apply focusing and noticing to each one. You can *notice* what you are concerned about. You can give those thoughts and feelings an empathetic audience. You can tolerate them without trying to fix them (because you can't) and then, when you choose, you can give yourself permission to let those thoughts go, and instead focus on your circle of influence.

Accepting when you can't

It is important to note that no matter how enlightened and awesome you are, no matter how fairly you should be treated, people still have the prerogative to be a dick if they so choose. This does not have to be a reflection on you. Start in your circle of influence by being an awesome human. You can radiate awesomeness and hope it will positively impact others, but remember, you don't get to decide how other people will receive your awesomeness. Some may find it inspiring, enriching or nourishing but they may find it threatening or patronising. Both are a choice made by those in your world which reflects how they see you, *but* they have made their choice based on their own values and circumstances over which you have zero control. And they probably won't know they are making a choice (to find your behaviour threatening, for example), because they haven't read this book.

You don't get to choose how people receive you, but you do get to decide what to do in response. You get to decide to live life by *your* values, which is pretty much what Victor Frankl said. In other words, don't be a dick, and don't become the dick just because everyone else around you appears to be. If you do, you are giving away power by allowing their bad behaviour to dictate yours. You're better than that.

When I was preparing to deploy to Iraq for the first time, one of the training courses I had to do was called 'Resistance to Interrogation'. It involves running around a soggy Dartmoor, freezing your tits off and starving while 'baddies' try and catch you. Eventually they do catch you, of course, after which you are interrogated and tortured. The instructors put you into stress positions for hours on end, they carry out mock executions, taunt you and play endless mind games. It feels pretty real, and it feels pretty unpleasant. The main thing we all took away from that exercise was, 'Don't ever get caught!' But I also took something else away. I knew that one of the first things that would happen when I was captured was that I'd be ordered to strip to my underwear. I had decided (a tad impulsively) to wear my favourite superhero underpants especially for this reason. I think I hoped it would deflect some of the attention away from my personal attributes and offer temporary relief from the verbal abuse that I knew was inevitable. It worked. My captors were jeering as I began undressing, but when my superhero pants were revealed, they stopped in their tracks. Their jaws hit the floor and they were momentarily speechless. One of them was fighting the urge to laugh. I remember thinking, 'You can decide when I eat, when I sleep, even when I go for a poo. But you don't get to decide what pants I put on this morning.' And as I stood shivering in a grey concrete cell, I felt powerful.

The key to feeling powerful is to keep exercising choices, even if it's something as trivial as what superhero underpants to wear (I recommend having a range of them). By standing tall and proud in my silly pants, for a moment, those instructors felt my power. They even felt something they didn't expect to feel. Humour. I think the key to happiness is for *everyone* to feel powerful. We should find and own our power and others will follow our lead.

Not disempowering others

Owning your power isn't an invitation to disempower others (though it's understandable to feel a smug sense of achievement when we get one over someone who's been a total prat to us). Sadly, that smug feeling only provides temporary relief, and often results in longer-term pain due to the inevitable games of one-upmanship that will follow. So own your power. Bask in that warm glow for sure. Forgive yourself if you take just a tiny bit of pleasure in it, but don't use it as a weapon to make others feel small. Use it as a weapon to help others to feel big.

Key takeaways from Chapter Six

- We need to stay mindful of choice – it is easy to lapse into 'victim mindset'.

- Victim mindset is not from laziness or weakness; it is ultimately due to a lack of self-worth.

- If circumstances are conducive to victim mindset, we would do well to go easy on ourselves, accept what we can't change and gently refocus our energy on what we can change.

- Responsibility sets us free. We always have a choice.

7

Choose To Fly Higher

I know what you're thinking. 'Wow, Sarah's really got this all figured out. She must have the perfect life. I bet she never has a bad day.' (It's helpful if you imagine me being impishly playful as I say this.) Well, yeah, you got me. I do feel blessed a lot of the time. But I also feel wretched, sad, scared and angry. I raise my voice at my son. (OK, let's be real, I shout at him.) I recently scowled at the lady ahead of me in the Waitrose queue for taking ages to count out her change. (Who uses cash these days, anyway?) I get annoyed at cute little dogs yapping excitedly, and sometimes I 'accidentally' walk on my partner's shins as I get out of bed because his snoring is keeping me awake.

I do these things because, like everybody else, I experience the full, glorious range of emotions, from pleasant to unpleasant, and these emotions are often powerful. It's true that I've learned to have a different relationship with these emotions and so I generally feel more confident, happier, more in control and more at peace. But I still feel them, even if I don't want to, and that's OK because I'm not a robot, and neither are you. If you were, you wouldn't need to read this book.

You are never going to stop getting hurt

Some of the most common questions I get asked by my clients are:

- How do I stop feeling like an imposter?
- How do I stop getting hurt?

I've got some bad news. You won't stop getting hurt. You won't stop worrying you're not enough and that's because you're not a robot and you feel things, which is OK. Let's get one thing clear. Your emotions aren't going anywhere, and really, you don't want them to. In this chapter I'm going to revisit how you can change your relationship with difficult emotions so that you can feel stronger.

You may recall Janet's story in Chapter Five. The key message there was that we can learn to sit with our pain and be our own empathetic witness, which can help us to feel stronger and more self-reliant in adversity. Let's take this concept and apply it to the most unpleasant and debilitating emotion of them all: fear. 'Why?' you may ask. So that we can not only do the things that scare us; we can get excited by them. We can feel bombproof. We can choose to fly higher.

Sitting with fear makes you stronger

Did you know that we are only born with two fears? The fear of falling and the fear of loud noises.[32] This goes a long way to explain why we generally don't fall out of bed while we are asleep (and why loud people can be so hard to trust).

We should remember that fear, like any emotion, exists to keep us alive. Fear tells us to run away from something dangerous. That being the case, ignoring it and serenely 'sitting with fear' would be the caveman equivalent of meditating next to an angry lioness that you've just separated from her cubs. It would be suicide. It's not difficult to understand why we often go to extraordinary lengths to avoid fear and the things we are afraid of. The problem though, is that in the modern world, fear is increasingly related to something that won't kill us, no matter how scary. An impending performance review, for example, might be scary, but you'll live through it.

Interestingly – and following on from my earlier point about only being born with two fears – we have learned most fears we have today. If you think about it, babies aren't born thinking, 'I wonder if I'll be loved? Am I enough? What if I'm not perfect?' You may recall that we covered this in Chapter Three: we learn to be afraid of failure, rejection, what other people think and so on. We've even come up with some trendy names for them, presumably to make them more available and memorable: imposter syndrome, perfectionism,

---

32   EJ Gibson and RD Walk, 'The "visual cliff"', *Scientific American*, 202/4 (1960), pp64–71; N Kounang, 'What is the science behind fear', *CNN Health* (29 October 2015), https://edition.cnn.com/2015/10/29/health/science-of-fear/index.html, accessed 25 July 2022

competitiveness and, the worst of them all, fear of missing out (FOMO).

This is not your fault. The truth is, we are all inevitably going to develop some form of limiting belief throughout our childhood, because when we are young, our prefrontal cortex isn't yet fully developed (that doesn't happen until our mid-twenties), so all those childhood disappointments – being dumped, not getting into the hockey team, messing up your driving test – create fertile breeding ground for developing hyper-investments.

What is a hyper-investment? It is what our brain manufactures to ensure that we do not endure repeated experiences of failure or rejection. It can manifest as follows: obsession with winning, being in control, perfectionism, cleanliness, mastery – actions that help us avoid repeating the experience of failure. If we are more afraid of rejection, our hyper-investment will present itself as an obsession with beauty (our own), people-pleasing, approval, intimacy and being chosen. The point is, we've learned to be afraid of things that won't kill us. And because we are afraid of them, we devote huge reserves of our energy avoiding them.

Fear is a mental construct which can be debilitating

So the first thing to take away is this: our fear is a mental construct that we can, well, kind of ignore a lot of the time. Ignoring our fear is not to be confused with being in denial or pushing it away – that just feeds it more. (This is because of Newton's third law which basically states that for every force, there is an equal and opposite force.[33] So, by resisting something, we simply get into a power struggle in our own heads. Bloody nightmare.)

I remember when I was learning how to night-fly a helicopter. If you want to know what that's like, imagine driving your car in the dark and then turning all the lights off. No headlamps. No street lights. Then imagine they put two tubes of toilet roll on your head and over your eyes. When you look through these toilet rolls, you can see something which looks a bit like the outside world except it's green and twinkly (a little bit like that scene in *The Matrix* when Neo can suddenly see in code). Unlike the movie though, this ability to see in green does not give us the superpower of dodging bullets. It just makes the experience weird. You can see what is directly in front of you in a slightly trippy version of reality and, for added fun, you can't see anything more than about twenty degrees either side of straight ahead, which means you must look with your neck rather than your eyes (rather like when dogs get those lampshade-style cones put around their necks to stop them scratching).

The toilet tubes on your face weigh 5 kg, which is equivalent to five large bags of sugar. (Try this if you like, and if you do, please send me a photo.) If we refer to Newton's law – every force attracts an equal and opposite force – this 5 kg weight on the front of your head is going to tilt your helmet forward unless you counterbalance it. To help with this counterbalance,

---

33   'Newton's laws of motion', *Encylopaedia Britannica* (no date), www.britannica.com/science/Newtons-laws-of-motion/Newtons-second-law-F-ma, accessed 9 June 2022

the powers-that-be have thoughtfully put another five bags of sugar on the back of your helmet, which means it feels like you are balancing a small microwave on your head. Seriously.

So back to flying that helicopter and our comparison of driving on the road with no car or street lights. Imagine there is no road (because that's the reality) and you're just hanging there in mid-air, OK? And there might not be a road, but the trees, ditches and walls on either side of the road still exist, which means it's vitally important you stay in this tiny bit of nothingness unless you want to crash and die. Your limited field of view means you must pick markers in the clearing. You might choose a tree that is straight ahead as a point of reference. That's your 12 o'clock marker. Then you pick a little bush off to your right. That's your 3 o'clock marker. Then you spot something that you can see through the bubble window next to your feet (yes, they have windows next to our feet) and that is known as – wait for it – the 2 o'clock daisy. Told you it was trippy. To keep yourself from crashing into the trees in the clearing, you have to stay dead centre. This means you have to keep all three markers in your field of view, but because of these toilet tubes, you can only see what is directly ahead, so you have to keep moving your microwave-heavy head from 12 o'clock, to 3 o'clock, to 2 o'clock.

It goes a bit like this. Look at the 12 o'clock marker. Keep it in your field of view a second or so to make sure it's not creeping away from you. If it's moving, do something with your hands and legs until it stops moving, then look at the 3 o'clock marker. Repeat the previous process. Then the 2 o'clock marker. Repeat the previous process. Then back to the 12 o'clock. At this point you are praying like hell that the tree you selected as your 12 o'clock marker is in the same place you left it. In my case, it often wasn't. If that happens, you must resist the urge to cry while you try to put the tree back where you left it without massively overreacting and charging into another tree on the other side of the clearing.

People often think of pilots as these effortlessly cool war heroes (or so I'm told), but if you could see me flying a helicopter in a clearing at night, the vision would be a lot less flattering. I would be sweating, hyperventilating a little, I would have my tongue stuck out in concentration, a death grip on the controls, and my aircraft would be bucking around underneath me like a demonic bronco as I swooped and swerved my way from corner to corner of the clearing. That's what it's like trying to land a helicopter in the middle of a forest clearing in the dead of night. In other words, it's bloody terrifying.

That's not the point of the story, though. I remember once flying with one of those guys who was irritatingly good at it. He seemed to find it so easy. He also had a remarkable ability to casually dispense profound bits of wisdom like they were vouchers at a DFS sofa sale. I remember asking him,

'Why is it *so* hard to fly at night?' He looked at me quizzically for a moment, as if checking he had heard this ludicrous question correctly. Eventually he responded.

'Sarah, the aircraft doesn't know it's dark.' In other words, it isn't actually more difficult to fly at night. Well, it is a bit harder, for all the reasons I've just explained. It's just that I had made it substantially more difficult for myself by being scared of the dark – and possibly microwaves.

You often fear things that won't kill you

Your brain will construct elaborate reasons why you should feel afraid of something when the truth is it has no more power over you than an irritating spot on your chin. Indeed, most pilots I have spoken to about this will admit that the thing that scared them most about night flying wasn't crashing and dying, it was crashing and looking stupid. As with the fear of night flying, you can pick it, squeeze it, fuss with it and make it way worse, or you can accept it's there and go out and be fabulous anyway.

Consider these two key points:

1. Fear, like any emotion, is transient. Everything passes. No matter how overwhelming and permanent it feels in the moment, it always passes. So if you do absolutely nothing at all, the feeling will diminish. In other words, you can tolerate it.

2. Fear isn't going anywhere. You are stuck with it, but it often feels a lot worse than it really is. Because of your childhood disappointments, you have learned to be afraid of things that won't kill you, which means you can probably do the things you are afraid of and you'll live. Thus, you can afford to change your response to fear. Instead of being hostage to fear, you can acknowledge it and then crack on, without giving it further attention. This is the beauty of training the mind. Once you master the basics, you can reapply them in more advanced or scary scenarios. It's pretty cool, really.

It is absolutely possible to change your response to fear so that you can do the things that scare you. Moreover, when you start to do the things that scare you, you might realise that not only will they not kill you, but they're kind of useful. I learned to have a completely different relationship with rejection (my biggest nemesis). Now, not only does it scare me less, but I get quite excited by it.

Why rejection is actually awesome

Rejection allows you to make ethical decisions based on your values

Rejection is kind of magic. There are times I have been rejected that I am truly proud of – for example, when I stood up to some pilots who were complaining about being asked to 'chill out' for the day before going and rescuing a hostage. I don't regret that decision. I'm proud I had the courage to do so, even though it made me unpopular. If you think about it, rejection can often mean that you stood up for your beliefs, and that, quite frankly, is going to mean a lot more to you on your deathbed than how many Instagram likes you accrued over the years. When you can tolerate rejection, what you are really saying is, 'I am enough, even if you don't love me.'

Rejection strengthens relationships

I also made a fantastic discovery about rejection that changed my thought process. Giving people permission to reject you is also a sign of respect to them, because effectively what you're saying is, 'You are enough, even if you don't love me.' When

I reflect, I realise this is true for those pilots who grumbled behind my back. I still respected them, even though they disagreed with me. I didn't *need* them to be my best friend for me to see their value. I can form my own opinion about someone and it doesn't need to rely on what they think about me. Of course, you want to be liked, but guess what? It doesn't mean everything. You can tolerate being disliked. You can tolerate being rejected and when you give people permission to reject you, far from weakening the relationship, you are strengthening it, because you are giving them the space to stand up for what they believe in.

Rejection is essential for growth

Perhaps the reason I was rejected in my hostage story is because the crews felt undervalued. After all, no matter how much I wanted to save that hostage, I still had a duty of care to my troops to make sure they were safe too. Perhaps they would have responded better if, rather than me telling them what to do, I had simply asked them the question, 'Do you think this can be done safely?' It's all about learning and growth.

Rejection is great for brand building

In the early days of my business, I got plenty of practice at being rejected. Inevitably some prospects would lose interest or decide I wasn't the right fit, or I would encounter resistance to what I was saying on social media. I learned a valuable lesson that continues to serve me well: rejection helps you to fine-tune your tribe/avatar/USP/prospect/niche, etc. When people decide you're not the right fit for them, they're saving you a huge chunk of valuable time and helping you to refine who your 'ideal person' is.

Of course it's not black and white. Sometimes it's not the right time. Sometimes we find it hard to see past a bad first impression. We are all human, after all. We also don't have to suddenly annex our friends because they've rejected us on occasion. Rejection can be temporary. Rejection simply means that in that moment, our needs and values do not align. That misalignment might last five minutes. It might last five years. It might last a lifetime. Either way, rejection is incredibly useful to us as leaders, as professionals and as humans. It can shine a spotlight, not just onto our own needs and values, but the needs and values of those we care about too. Learn to love rejection, and not only will you feel happier and stronger, you'll also be the most infuriatingly congenial human on the planet.

How to tackle the fear of rejection

Here's what the fear of rejection might look like: 'I'm afraid that if I show up authentically, I'll be rejected.' You now know that you can tolerate fear, so an appropriate response might be: 'Yes, I am afraid, and that's OK, because this fear won't kill me.' Three important things are going on here. First, you are acknowledging the fear, rather than pushing it away. Second, you are forgiving yourself for feeling this fear (it's OK not to feel OK...) and third, you're reminding yourself that this is a mental construct and the feeling itself won't kill you.

You can also 'JFDI' – just fucking do it. You do what feels right, even if you don't feel like doing it. Every time you show up as you, even when you are scared, you are training your brain that you can tolerate fear and not be held hostage to this feeling. Over time, you'll start to feel more in control of your behaviour in the presence of fear, and that's when you need to keep going. Eventually you'll realise that you haven't even noticed the fear and you're doing a damn good job at being authentically you, with all the confidence of a four-year-old wearing a Batman T-shirt.

Then you can learn from the outcome. Usually, we either exaggerate how awful the outcome will be, or we minimise how well-equipped we are at dealing with it. If you are rejected though, the truth is, you'll live, and you can use the outcome to learn and grow. I did. I've got *lots* of personal experience of rejection. I was not the cool kid at school. I was geeky, unfashionable and focused on being in the RAF, which meant I was probably not the most fun to be around. We've discussed already that those formative years in school set the conditions for our hyper-investment of choice, which for me was definitely a fear of rejection. Then I decided to join a male-dominated organisation, which almost guaranteed that I would never completely fit in. That didn't stop me from trying though. I swore more often, I had casual sex, I drank beer and did lots and lots of press-ups, just so I could be 'one of the boys', so that I could avoid feeling that sting of rejection, but of course underneath it all, I was still me. I was, and still am, a passionate and sensitive person.

When I left the RAF, I quickly realised that no matter how much I disliked social media, I needed to embrace it for my new business. I half-heartedly started posting on LinkedIn, being careful that I didn't become a humble bragger, a sycophant or controversial. I certainly didn't want to be judged or found wanting. I didn't want to be rejected, which ultimately meant I didn't want to evoke any kind of emotional response from people who saw my posts. When I finally began to be more 'honest' about my beliefs (I posted something about victim mindset), I was rewarded. In fact, I gained my first big customer from one such post. He said:

> 'I know I need to look after staff wellbeing but I'm worried they are going to use it as an excuse for poor behaviour – I get the sense you can help me without giving the business a soft underbelly.'

The point is, trying to be someone you're not just doesn't work. I put this mask on every day to try and be like 'them', which made me brittle and uptight. Fighting with my fear of rejection did me no favours whatsoever. In fact, it often made me more miserable. I wasn't being genuine around those guys, which was undermining my self-esteem, and, despite the big act, I was still being rejected. The result? I felt deflated and pissed off. The answer is *not* to try and resist or avoid rejection, it's to lean into it.

How to practise rejection without becoming a dick

My final offering is to flip the premise of rejection and share how it's possible for you to reject people without becoming a dick. As I said, often the biggest barrier to achieving our full potential is being able to say no to other people. We are hardwired to be part of a tribe, so we will always feel a strong urge to be accepted and validated by others. We also have a culture in which letting others down can be seen as a real dick move. I saw this in the RAF. We had a 'can do' culture which meant that we would always try to achieve the impossible. We would always try to say yes. I'm super-proud of that culture. I love how forward-leaning our organisation was, but I also saw how limiting it could be. High-ranking, confident and capable people could be crippled by the idea of saying no. I think they would rather have been mortared or shot at than let the team down, but sometimes, you have to say no to do the right thing. Sometimes, you need to tolerate other people's disappointment to help them grow.

Think about raising a child. The job of the parent is not to be indispensable. The job of a parent is to be dispensable, to give their child the skills to stand on their own two feet, because the truth is, we won't all be around forever. Our children won't be able to look after themselves if they get molly-coddled all their life. At some point, maybe it's when your child asks, 'Can you tie my shoelaces?' or, 'Can you help me with my homework?' or some other variant of this, you have to say no. Not because you don't want to help them, but so that they can learn it themselves. Then they will realise that they don't need you, which makes you dispensable. It might not feel like it, but becoming dispensable to our children is an act of true love. It applies equally well to our colleagues, our team mates or our employees.

I recently met a man who proudly declared himself a 'compulsive helper'. The phrase resonated with me. I think lots of us would love to describe ourselves as that, don't you? But think for a second about what it really means. It means we *have* to help others, and if we're honest, that's usually because of how it makes us feel. We want to feel valuable. We want to feel needed. We can't bear to see others in pain while they work stuff out for themselves, so we try to do something to reduce their pain and bear it ourselves. It's not easy to step back and let others muddle their way through, but if we really want to help, then we need to become aware of our own agenda and put it aside. We need to come to terms with our own circle of concern.

How other people tackle their life problems is something that will always concern us, for sure, but it's not something we can dictate. It's universally acknowledged that we learn best when we learn it for ourselves, 'learn from our mistakes' as it were, so being a caring and supportive team leader/parent/partner/ colleague is about creating a safe space for other people to do their own learning. And sometimes that means saying no. You don't have to be a total monster about it of course. I shared some tips in Chapter Two as to how you can let people down gently, but it's worth repeating one here: 'I can't help you with this right now, but I have some time at X,' and then give them the space to go and figure it out for themselves. See how they grow. See how they start to feel a bit taller and a bit more confident. You see, I told you rejection was awesome!

The root cause of our fears

The bottom line: our fears usually come from a limiting belief. Maybe fear of rejection isn't your thing. Maybe it's fear of failure, or being hurt, or feeling powerless or insignificant. There seems to be no shortage of fears our brains will produce, so you might be thinking, 'Great, but how does this apply to my fear?' But when it comes down it, we really have one fear. When I learned to sit with my fears, I realised that underneath it all, I was terrified that I wasn't enough. During my subsequent years studying the mind, I've come to the sad, but oddly comforting, conclusion that most people worry they are not enough. It often manifests itself as a limiting belief: 'I am not enough.' Most human beings that I have met, when you drill down far enough, have this belief in some form or another. Which is great news, because if we know what the problem is then we can do something about it.

Now you could, of course, try and change that belief. You could write down a new belief. You could chant it every morning to yourself. You could write it on your mirror in your favourite lippy. If that works for you, then knock yourself out. But if you're anything like me, it takes more than a sweep of lippy to reverse forty-odd years of learned thinking patterns. This is a hardwired belief. I wonder if it is inevitable that we will always believe this in some form, because it is human nature to strive for excellence, to evolve, to improve. You could argue that this belief serves us in some ways, because it means we don't become complacent, but are always growing. We are a work in progress. And that's OK. If you recall from Chapter Five, there is a danger that trying to change our beliefs can end up with us wrestling with them, which can make the situation worse.

I recommend a different approach. The good news is, we don't need to try and change the belief. We can simply change our relationship with the fear that feeds it. For example, if you believe you are not enough, then you will probably be afraid to show up as yourself in case you are rejected or you fail. What we've learned, though, is that there is a way to change our relationship with that fear: you can tolerate it and JFDI. Two things are happening when you do this:

1. Every time you tolerate a difficult feeling, you realise you are stronger and braver than you thought.

2. Every time you JFDI, you are training your brain that you are not hostage to your feelings. Just because you *believe* it, doesn't mean you have to *be* it.

I realised it was possible to go out and be unapologetically me in the presence of this fear and in the full knowledge it might result in me being rejected. I was showing up in a way that felt right to me, even though it scared me. You can do that too. When you do, you are creating new evidence for a better belief. And over time, guess what? You have a new belief. One day, your new belief might even be, 'Today, I am enough.' Ta-dah!

I know I said I'm not one for chanting, but the meditation below allows you to understand your limiting belief without judgement. Often the thing that stops us letting go of our self-sabotaging thoughts and beliefs is permission – we find it hard to give ourselves permission to go easy on ourselves and forgive ourselves for being human. If that resonates, then this meditation is for you. Remember, just because you believe it, doesn't mean you have to be it.

Meditation: Limiting beliefs

Read through the following instructions several times or listen to the guided meditation on Soundcloud at https://soundcloud.com/user-978445649 – 'Lim belief med'.

- Start by focusing on your breath for a few minutes and centring yourself.

- Let your limiting belief rest in your awareness. If it hasn't come up, gently recall it now.

- Observe it for a while. Notice any feelings that come up for you or any temptation to resist it. There is no right or wrong. You are just letting yourself experience this belief fully in a conscious and compassionate way.

- Embrace it as you already have in your life so far. It's not good or bad. It's just part of your story. If you find this difficult, then say to yourself, 'It's OK not to like this. It's OK not to be OK.'

- Now shift your attention into your body so that you can become aware of any physical sensations that are coming up for you.

- Give yourself permission to feel the full energy of this belief.

- Now explore the external factors that have contributed to this belief. Your upbringing, relationships, other people, experiences. There's no need to get involved with the story here. Just notice where the external energy had fuelled your belief.

- Give yourself permission to let go of the energy that belongs to external factors. Release it back into the world. If it helps, you can say, 'Thank you, but I don't need you now.'

- Now become aware of your own, powerful energy that's been obscured by the external energy. Reclaim it. Reclaim that self-compassion and power that is rightfully yours. Let it bathe you in a warm glow. Feel it fill every cell in your body.

- Finally, say to yourself, 'I am [insert your belief here].'

Summary

Human beings are magnificent. Our minds are a complex labyrinth of neural pathways that have limitless permutations in the way they can interact. This means that while we are basic and primed for survival, we are also gloriously complex. Underneath it all, we all experience fear. What's brilliant is that we don't have to wrestle with it, push it away or fuel it. We can learn to tolerate it and then, in the presence of fear, go out and be awesome anyway.

At the start of this book, I talked about the swan as a metaphor for life. Life often throws us curveballs. It can get pretty rough out there, but like the swan, we have a choice. We can choose to sink or swim. This book is about flying. And fly you will, because you are a swan. One day, simply because you chose to keep swimming, you'll realise you are stronger than you ever knew you could be. When you have that, it's not so much that you're fearless – it's something better than that. You have something that everyone else wants. You have self-belief. When that happens... Well, then you're flying – and you can fly even higher.

Key takeaways from Chapter Seven

- Fear is transient. We can choose to tolerate it and let it pass.

- Many fears such as fear or failure or rejection are learned from our childhood experiences and are not as awful as we think. We can do the things that scare us, and we'll probably live.

- Rejection is often not as permanent or as awful as we think it will be. In fact, it is essential in leadership and can strengthen relationships.

- Our fears drive our limiting beliefs – eg 'I am not enough.' We don't need to fight this belief. We can simply change how we respond to the fear that drives it, go out there and be awesome in the presence of fear, and create the evidence for a better belief.

Conclusion

The last seven chapters have been a journey, a journey that I hope you have come on with me. It's a journey to explore how the mind works and, crucially, how to get it working for you even when you're in your own version of a battlefield.

I wanted to bring it all together by sharing one last piece of wisdom that I've learned: no one's looking at you.

I don't mean that to sound harsh, but the truth is we are wired for survival, which means we are wired to look out for number one. No one is looking at you even half as much as you imagine them to be. I personally find that thought and realisation helpful. It makes it easier not to take everything so goddamn personally, because if feeling wounded by others was a national sport, I'd be a gold medallist by now. Take it from me. This is good news.

It means that when people behave towards you in a way that you don't like, at least half of that is to do with their narrative, their beliefs and their values. If you've learned nothing else, remember that most people believe they are not enough, which means their behaviour is often driven by fear: fear of looking stupid, fear of being insignificant, fear of being worthless, fear of being a monster, fear of being hurt, fear of loss, fear of powerlessness... These are all fears that human beings experience, and which drive our behaviour. Fear is powerful, so whatever someone has just said or done, it's unlikely to be entirely about you.

Understanding that you're not being noticed anywhere near as much as you think you are means you can go out there and be yourself. If you make a tit of yourself, the chances are a lot less people will notice than you think. Even if they do notice, they'll move on quickly, so take this an invitation to be unapologetically you, safe in the knowledge that the person this will have the most impact on, is you.

As we discussed earlier, we often learn the most valuable lessons from totally fucking things up, and I think we would do well to remember that. Sometimes it feels like the current culture is teaching us to be disproportionately inward-looking and to avoid difficulty. We see it as a weakness, as something we simply can't tolerate. It's always all about us, isn't it? About how fragile we are feeling. How wronged we feel. How overwhelmed we are. We believe it's someone else's fault, and so it's someone else's problem to fix. Feeling sorry for ourselves doesn't help anyone.

It's time to realise, in the nicest possible way, that it's not about you. Believe me, I say this with considerable experience, and absolutely no judgement. I spent a lot of time thinking it was all about me and it caused me untold amounts of agony. The truth is that when you make it all about you, what you're really doing is getting in your own way, so I'm saying this with love: it's time to start looking outwards and realise that everyone else has got their shit going on and that they want to feel loved too. They are just as scared as you are – and you can help.

You might say, 'But wait a minute Sarah, you just said no one is looking at me, so how do I make the world a better place?' Good point. I'll tell you how. People will look at you when there's something in it for them. Remember, that's how we are wired, so they will look at you when you have something they want, and in my experience, what most people want is permission: permission to forgive themselves for being human, permission to strive for more, permission to be different, permission to be wrong, permission to be right. When you go out there and be awesomely you, make a total hash of it from time to time and keep smiling anyway. When you do that, you give others permission to do the same.

Fear is contagious and so is courage. Do you know what else? When you start looking outwards, you may find the inner critic becomes a bit quieter. (Remember, our attention can only be in one place at a time.) You may even find that you don't need to fix anything after all, you simply needed to change your focus. One day, you'll wake up and realise that your inner narrative has changed. Your narrative is no longer, 'I am not enough.' Now you're telling yourself, 'I am enough,' and believing it – because it's true. You are enough. And now *you're* the one teaching people to fly higher. Go get 'em, tiger.

Acknowledgements

I wrote this book because I wanted to help other people like me to get through the tough times. It's because I came through my own tough times that I'm now able to help others. But I didn't do it on my own. I want to thank all the people that helped me when I was struggling. I know that I was often lost in my own little world of pain, and it sometimes blinded me to the kindness that surrounded me. So many people helped me on my journey to putting myself back together. So many people were kind and good. I'm sorry it took me so long to see it. I won't be able to do them all justice, but here are some people I'd like to give special thanks to: Miriam, my dad, Jamie and Aileen, my ex-husband Andrew, DH, Becks, Ria, Claire, Emily, Andy Mac and the team at CoAST.

My gratitude also goes to AnnMarie Wyncoll, my book coach who helped me get the message right, to convey my personality and wit (!) without being too offensive or confusing. Thank you to Mindy and her team for getting this book into print.

Thanks to John Peters, who has been generous with his time and advice, mentored me and inspired me to become a speaker and author. Also, to Mandy Hickson, who graciously encouraged me to copy her lead as a female pilot speaker and author. And to Maria Franzoni, who helped me get onto the big stage and told me, 'All the best speakers have written a book – when are you writing yours?'

Thanks to my mother Helen, who will never read this book but taught me some of the biggest lessons that are shared within it. It was my mum who taught me to be brave. It was my mum who believed I could achieve my dreams. And it was my mum who ultimately taught me how to fly. She often remarked that she wanted to be remembered when she was gone. I think it worried her. This is what I would say to her if I could. 'Mum, you needn't have worried. You are inimitable and I miss you more than I ever thought possible. You will never be forgotten.'

Thank you to Tim, my partner-in-crime, who has been with me on this journey; whom I have learned with, laughed with and cried with. It's been one hell of a ride. One thing I am most grateful for about us – we never gave up when it got hard. We bloody well fought for each other.

Finally, thank you to my son Arthur, my little ray of sunshine, who inspires me every day.

The Author

Sarah Furness is an ex-helicopter pilot in the RAF, mindfulness coach and motivational speaker. During her experiences, both at war and at home, she learned that tough capable people don't always feel as strong as they look. She includes herself in that number. This led her to develop the Healthy Automatic Behaviours In Threatening Scenarios (HABITS) formula – a blend of mindfulness and military combat techniques that can be used to train the mind to be bombproof under pressure and feel awesome at the same time.

She has a young son whom she adores and who inspires her every day. She is planning her future world tour with her partner and son.

🌐 www.sarahfurness.com

🌐 www.wellbeitcoach.com

💼 @sarahjfurness

📘 @wellbeitcoach

📷 @wellbeitcoach